Many Moons

A SONGWRITER'S MEMOIR

SONGWRITER SERIES

Many Moons

A SONGWRITER'S MEMOIR

DAYNA MANNING

BlueMoon
PUBLISHERS

Many Moons: A Songwriter's Memoir

ISBN: 978-1-988279-89-3

Editor: Allister Thompson

Book Designer: Jamie Arts

Cover Photo by Dave Brosha

Published in Stratford, Canada, by Blue Moon Publishers.

Printed and bound in Canada.

The author greatly appreciates you taking the time to read this work. Please consider leaving a review wherever you bought the book, or telling your friends or blog readers about *Many Moons: A Songwriter's Memoir* to help spread the word. Thank you for your support.

CONTENTS

"Ain't it funny how the past takes the better memories last, 'cause the pain fades away, it all fades away."

— Stan Rogers

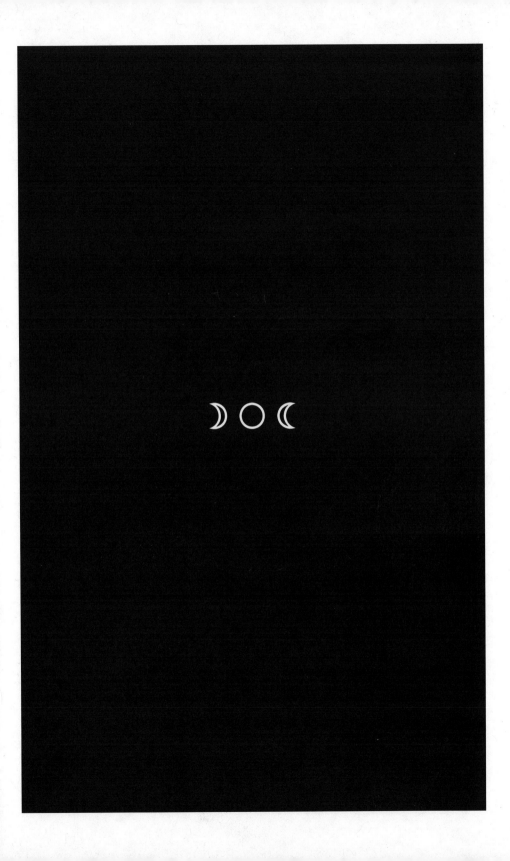

FOREWORD

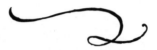

Dayna's lyrical tales of music and life are fresh, honest, and a study guide to every singer-songwriter. This book took me effortlessly across Canada and into her music itself. Count me as a member of Dayna's Folk Army!

— Chris Hadfield, astronaut and fellow musician

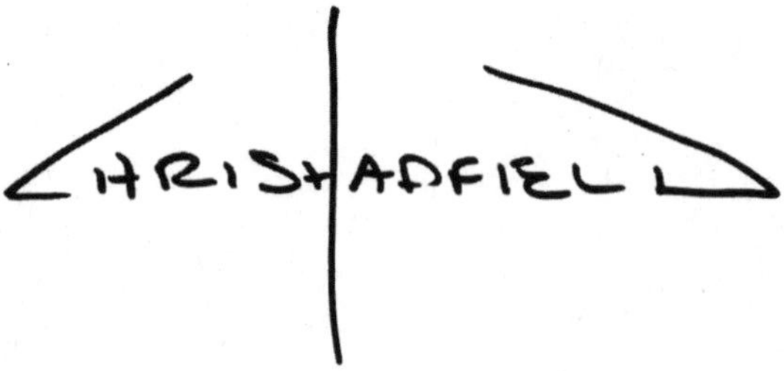

To my Mom and Dad

And to my students as they set out on their own musical adventures, may the songs take you places you have never imagined.

INTRODUCTION

As I sit in the sunroom of a century-old farmhouse in the middle of County Clare, Ireland, looking out over crooked stone walls and deep green fields, with the Atlantic glistening in the sun on the horizon, I can only reflect on how fortunate I am. It's day six of this particular adventure, and the umbrella has turned out to be the most useless item in my luggage.

I am travelling with deeply creative, musical friends on this trip, all decades apart in age. We are enjoying playing music each night at sessions in the surrounding towns, with locals and folks attracted here from all over the world by the music. We have made instant new friends of all ages, from far and wide, simply by sharing a song.

My experience here is reflective of the life that music has blessed me with. Time and again, I've watched rooms full of people keeping to their own circles become instantly joined with strangers for an evening, a week, a year, and even a lifetime by one person sharing a song. A song instantly invites a connection to a point of view, an emotion, a heartache. It makes strangers start conversations based on a feeling of normalcy. It leads to the next song.

I didn't truly understand the power of song when I penned my first one at sixteen. I mean, I knew how connected my soul felt to songs I heard on the radio and television, but I had no idea of their power in real life

back then. As soon as I wrote "A Walk on the Moon," it was as if my life became a choose-your-own-adventure book, in which each door was opened by a song.

Little did I know that this book would be so very easy to write! When I thought about each song and the particular adventures it took me on, the stories were so splendid, and I was so excited to share them, that I could hardly stop writing. I actually had to make many decisions about which tales to tell.

This book, a memoir told through my songs, is in chronological order, but one chapter may not necessarily run into the next.

The first half of the book spans my career attempting to navigate the music business. It covers my adventures exploring the Toronto open-stage scene as a teenager, finding a team of people around me who wanted me to succeed, and having my first album, *Volume 1*, recorded on a spec deal with a Toronto studio, picked up by EMI Music Canada.

We then head to California, where I had an opportunity to make my next album, *Shades*, with a major-label budget and my recording idol at the helm. I found myself bouncing around classic studios like Ocean Way and A&M and working beside the best in the business.

Through all of this time, I was still trying hard to find stability in my early adult life. I wanted a partner and security in my home life. At around chapter six, you can feel a shift in my desire to be a part of the commercial music business and a change in perspective and songwriting.

After moving to Northern British Columbia to pursue a serious relationship, I found a new connection with music deeply inspired by my surroundings and friends. I was working full-time to quell the desire for financial stability that I never had but found the daily connection to community and coworkers reinspired my songwriting like never before.

The formation of my Canadiana trio Trent Severn eventually led me back to Ontario and allowed me to continue to explore my love of storytelling through songwriting. The band would afford me the opportunity to develop my producing and engineering chops on our sophomore record, *Trillium*, and the following release, *Portage*.

I've stayed pretty focused on the positives in this book. There have been some very heartbreaking, hard times that come along with choosing this existence, but it's the great memories that prevail and I have chosen to share.

There has never been a moment where I considered giving up. I'm certain that the only thing actually required to be a singer-songwriter is an unwavering belief in yourself, which may possibly be the hardest part.

A WALK ON THE MOON

December 1994

A walk on the beach, a cool breeze in the night
You'll never discover the finer things in life
A million dollar baby and a million dollar wife

Today there's a heaven, tomorrow there's not
Five, six, and seven are tied in a knot
You stepped in the web and now you're caught

I meant to meet you in that small green room
With three chairs and a table, three forks and a spoon
Someday I'll take you for a walk on the moon
For a walk on the moon

Don't tell me who will stay or who will walk away
Don't tell me who to love, I'll love you anyway
I'll live my life the way I want to day by day

You have the power to stop the time
I fell down the hill in my nursery rhyme
You have your wisdom and I've learned mine

It is a symbol, the man's dress tie
A symbol of manhood in the dreams we pass by
I cannot stare you right in the eye

Don't tell me who will stay or who will walk away
Don't tell me who to love, I'll love you anyway
I'll live my life the way I want to day by day

Someday I'll take you for a walk on the moon

A WALK ON THE MOON

"A Walk on the Moon" is the first fully formed song I ever wrote. I certainly had no idea how it would absolutely change my entire life.

After studying piano and vocals throughout my youth, I started to play guitar at thirteen. I would attend back-to-back private lessons on nylon-string guitars with my father, David Manning. My dad is a fabulous trumpet player and high school music teacher, and he became interested in teaching guitar at school in the early nineties. At that time, students were losing interest in playing traditional concert band instruments, and the music program enrolment at Northwestern Secondary School in Stratford was declining. The guitar program my father started would remedy the lack of eager music students.

There was a big shift happening in popular music at that time. The angular, synthetic sound of the eighties was quickly becoming drowned out by the distorted guitars and edgy poetic lyrics of Nirvana, the Red Hot Chili Peppers, Pearl Jam, and Guns n' Roses. Kids were very interested in playing guitar, and my dad knew this was the instrument that could attract them back to studying music. By the time I entered grade nine in 1992, his guitar courses were established. He had even let his greying hair grow to his shoulders and wore it tucked in a ponytail like all the cool kids.

I remember the moment I was hooked on becoming a singer/songwriter. It was at our high school Remembrance Day ceremony, at which I was invited to play Bob Dylan's "Blowing in the Wind." We all go to new schools

for high school in Stratford, and I was navigating the tricky social scene that went with the change. I fingerpicked the chords on my classical guitar and sang the beautiful tune with all my might in front of the whole school. And it changed my life. In the days and weeks after, everyone started talking to me and saying hello in the halls, asking about where I learned to sing or play. Absolutely everyone. I didn't have to just hang out with the farm kids, the popular girls or the sports fanatics. Everyone seemed to be my new friend, or acquaintance at least, and right there was the best reason in the world to play music to me. An instant connection with my fellow humans.

That year I managed to join a band called Soylent Green my fellow classmates had formed (yes, named after the obscure seventies sci-fi film). We played a battle of the bands at the Mitchell District High School, which we lost to an incredible group from the nearby town of St. Marys called The Cause. They wrote their own tunes and were all-around great. The guitar player from that band would soon become my first boyfriend, and in time my first heartbreak, which would fuel my entry into song-writing and ultimately the music business.

I wrote "A Walk on the Moon" on December 3, 1994, freshly heartbroken. I was babysitting two young girls for a lovely fella named Dave Bates who was, and still is, very supportive of my guitar playing and singing around Stratford. His daughters Lisa and Laura were both in preschool at the time, and after I put them to bed, I grabbed Dave's guitar, and "A Walk on the Moon" wrote itself. It was done as fast as I could write it down. Both of Dave's daughters would grow up to be incredible violin players, and it was so neat to me that Laura, who I put to bed at six years old, just before I wrote my first song, would become the first fiddle player in my band Trent Severn almost twenty years later.

Anyhow, in the next few weeks, I penned a few more songs, and with "A Walk on the Moon" as my anchor, I recorded a four-song demo tape at a local studio with a kind fella named Andrew Flach. I started selling it to friends at school, photocopying the hand-drawn cassette sleeves and dubbing each tape myself in my bedroom.

Throughout high school, I also worked as a junior waitress and child caretaker at a new restaurant in Stratford called Hyacinth House. The

owners, a bohemian couple from Toronto, were both musical and had a three-year-old son. They lived upstairs at the restaurant on the southwest corner of Waterloo and Coburg Streets. When they split up, and the father returned to the big city, I was asked if I would be allowed to escort their son on the train to Toronto one weekend a month to visit his dad and various grandparents. They paid me well, and the family lived in nice neighbourhoods. The only time their child and I were alone together was on the train rides from Stratford to Union Station, where the family collected us swiftly. Once settled, no one seemed too concerned about what I wanted to do. In the evenings, I could do as I pleased, and with a key to the house in hand, I started exploring.

Unbeknownst to my parents, I would quickly seek out the weekly entertainment mags, *NOW* magazine and *EYE Weekly*, to plot my open-stage tours around the city. I played at any open stage I could. I would navigate the subway to the Free Times Cafe, the El Mocambo, I'd hit legendary guitarist Wild T's open stage at The Unicorn near Yonge and Eglinton, Bar None on the Danforth — anywhere I could manage getting to. Even though I was underage, when I walked into bars with my guitar in hand, no one asked any questions. I was always on my best behaviour and tried to introduce myself straight away. Looking back, I really don't know what compelled me to go to all these open stages, but I just felt like that was what I was supposed to be doing.

One Sunday night over March break in 1995, I worked up the nerve to go to the open stage advertised at Lee's Palace, the iconic rock club on Bloor. I had wanted to go for a while but usually wasn't in the city on Sundays. An incredible cover band called The Carpet Frogs were playing and hosting, and it seemed like the crowd was only there to listen to them. They were all killer players performing classic covers that broke into three-part harmony often and with ease. Jeff Jones from Tom Cochrane's Red Rider was even the bass player.

On their first break, I approached the lead singer, who had very long, wavy black hair and was as intimidating as any rock star I'd ever seen. I asked if I could play a few songs.

He set me up with a microphone for my guitar and one for my vocal

and went on his break. I played "A Walk on the Moon," and the entire room stood silently watching. I could even see that the two fellas playing pool at the back of the room had stopped their game to listen. It was a pretty cool feeling; Lee's Palace had turned into a coffee house where you could hear a pin drop for a few moments. It was one of those ineffable moments that happen in live music, the ones all us musicians crave, the ones that hook us for life. We've all made them happen, but we often don't know how exactly, and most of us spend our life trying to perfect them.

As I left the stage, the whole band introduced themselves, and I had made a few new friends. The intimidating singer, Nick Sinopoli, was as kind as could be. I found out he also fronted an Alice Cooper cover band, which suited his daunting guise.

I was then approached by a man named Ray Coburn. He said he was a musician too and seemed to be friends with the band. He looked like a rock star. He had buzzed short blond hair and was dressed head to toe in light denim. He wore heavy silver jewellery: earrings, a bracelet, and several rings. A long open wool trench coat and leather gloves kept him warm, and he had a small soul patch under his lower lip. He seemed interested in finding out more about my music and possibly helping me out.

Before I left that night, Nick also gave me a phone number for a lady named Sandy MacNevin. She had to leave right away, but I guess she told Nick that if I had written the song "A Walk on the Moon" to give me her phone number. Sandy was the entertainment director at a massive club in Kitchener called Lulu's Roadhouse. Lulu's was the size of a small shopping mall and once held the *Guinness Book of World Records* title for longest bar. Sandy also lived in Toronto and was friends with the band.

I gave Nick and Ray each a copy demo tape and my phone number. We have to keep in mind that I was giving them my parents' home phone number, since there were no cell phones in our pockets in 1995, and I was sixteen years old.

Both Sandy and Ray showed sincere concern for my well-being and future. Neither of them worked with young artists at the time, but they were both music industry vets in their early thirties and recognized that the business can be crazy to navigate, even with the best of intentions.

At the time, they didn't know each other and in the next few weeks would investigate one another to see if they were decent folk, which, lucky for me, they both were.

I met up with Sandy for lunch in Kitchener a few weeks later. My mom drove me to meet her, and we quickly struck up a friendship. She gave me an open invitation to attend concerts at Lulu's, and I was able to see many great shows there — B.B. King, Trooper, Burton Cummings — despite my admission-limiting age. I'd often travel with Sandy to Toronto after the shows and stay at her place as I started getting gigs of my own in Toronto.

I met Ray on my next babysitting trip to Toronto. I can remember that we went for a walk near where I was staying and sat in a park and talked. It must have been late April or so, because I recall dirty yellow grass and the extra gravel kicking around that comes with spring. He told me he was in a band called Honeymoon Suite, and I asked him if that was a local band, because I hadn't heard of them. In hindsight this was rather humorous, since they were in fact a very successful Canadian band with gold records, Juno Awards, and world tours behind them. Ray was an excellent keyboard and piano player and was really talented with programming and synthesizers. When I met him, he was playing in Alannah Myles's band. She was fresh off the fame of her hit song "Black Velvet."

Musically, Ray and I we were a match. He wasn't constrained by the ideas of musical genre or form, and I wasn't either. We ended up spending a lot of time together, sharing ideas, and despite our age gap, we became quite good friends. He lived in a duplex in the Beaches area of Toronto, and I would often stay there too, on the living room futon. I started travelling to Toronto more often, and he started finding me opening slots with bigger bands and introducing me to industry folks. I still found lots of time to hit the open stages and wander around on my own. I'd even busk on Queen Street in front of the Rivoli, where I'd make as much as $80 a sitting to keep my city trips afloat. Daniel Greaves, the singer from Winnipeg's kings of indie rock, The Watchmen, even put $20 in my case once, which made my entire teenage life at that time.

I continued writing a lot over the next year. I was endlessly inspired by

a record called *Wildflowers* by Tom Petty that came out in late 1994. I fell absolutely in love with that record and used it as a guiding light for writing the rest of my own. I looked at it as a reference tool, thinking, *Okay, this is how you do it. This is how you pace an album. This is how it should sound.*

Wildflowers had depth, variety, honesty, and grace. The impeccably written songs were captured with top-notch performances, production, and arrangements. I even thought the song sequence was flawless. While all my high school friends were obsessing over The Breeders and Green Day, I thought this relatively boring middle-aged blond guy made the best-sounding record I had ever heard, and it never left my side. I even kept an unopened backup CD copy in case I lost mine. *Wildflowers* went on to win the Grammy Award for Best Engineered Album, Non-Classical in 1996, which I took note of and would go on to make everyone working on my first recording reference.

Ray really wanted to produce me and struck up a speculation (or "spec") deal with his friend and studio owner/engineer Harold "Harry" Hess. Harry worked out of the small room of Phase One Studios in Toronto. The spec deal meant that everyone would only get paid if the record was bought by a major label. In 1995 we started recording tracks that would eventually become my first record, the aptly titled *Volume 1*. As I wrote more songs over the next year and a half, we would casually book studio time with Harry around his paying projects. We used the first four or five songs from those sessions as a better demo tape and started shopping it to record companies. An A&R rep from EMI Music Canada named Bonnie Fedrau became quite interested in what I was up to and started coming to any little show I had. This started a small buzz around me in the music industry.

Ray made appointments with Warner, Sony, EMI, and we would just head over on a weekday and I would play for their presidents and A&R teams in their boardrooms, all alone. I was even invited to play for the highly regarded label Private Music in L.A., which paid for an all-expenses trip to California while I was still in grade twelve. I think I have a million photos of the first hotel room I stayed in, at the famous Mondrian Hotel on Sunset Boulevard.

Things got pretty crazy around that time. I had missed more than

thirty days of high school that year, and the school refused to give me credits based on attendance, even though I had kept up on the workload. My three-credit enriched geography class was even built around an in-depth study of Los Angeles, and despite the fact that I was the only person in the class who had actually been there that year, the time didn't count. I would end up writing my General Education Development (GED) test shortly after.

During all this I had made a deep connection artistically with Deane Cameron, the president of EMI. He truly enjoyed my songs. When we finally had *Volume 1* recorded, he bought the record from us and signed me to a multi-album record deal shortly after I turned eighteen in 1996. This meant everyone who had volunteered to work on my album finally got paid. What an incredible experience it was to make what would end up being a major label album just the way I wanted to, surrounded by skilled musicians who believed in me at such a tender age. I am eternally grateful to Ray for this life-changing experience. It certainly takes a village.

Despite how well we worked together, Ray and I would have our moments battling in the studio over artistic production ideas. I always had ideas for the instrumentation that I had in mind when I wrote the songs and fought hard for some of them. In the end I officially produced one track on the record, titled "My Kind."

The month of March at Lee's Palace seemed lucky for me. In 1996, I had a solo gig there opening for Moe Berg's band, The Pursuit of Happiness, on Saturday, March 23rd. I sang a short set on my own, and the headlining band went on.

While securing a spot in the audience to watch TPOH, I was approached by a man just a bit older than me, with long, wavy hair and glasses. In the dark light of the club, I had initially mistaken him for a lady named Heather Pollock, who worked for TMP, "The Music Publisher," headed by Frank Davies, who had been courting me for a publishing deal, which I would eventually sign. I actually said hello and gave him a hug before I realized he wasn't Heather — how funny looking back. They clearly don't look alike.

He introduced himself as Sean, and we started chatting. The club

was just packed, and with the band playing, it was hard to see and hear each other. He said he was there from New York and came to Lee's Palace because he was playing a showcase there Monday night and wanted to check out the club. He wanted to know if I wrote my own tunes, particularly "A Walk on the Moon," and I told him I wrote them all. We really hit it off. We talked loudly for a good fifteen to twenty minutes before deciding to go next door for some food. We were both hungry and wanted to continue talking. I excused myself to use the washroom and to let Ray know where I'd be.

While I was washing my hands, a woman beside me at the sink asked about the young man I was talking to. I said his name was Sean and that he seemed really nice. I asked if she knew him. She said "Well, no — but he's John Lennon's son." I was shocked — I honestly had no idea. On my way back to find Sean again, I detoured to the bar to tell Ray I was going for a bite to eat — with Sean Lennon. I knew he would be excited. Ray has one tattoo: the iconic self-portrait illustration of John Lennon on his right shoulder. He gave me cash from his wallet and told me to pay for the meal.

I don't remember how we all ended up back at Ray's house that night, but we did. The timing of this event was so interesting to me. Back in Stratford, I had just painted my bedroom a bright yellow, and as I worked, I repetitively listened to a tape my dad made me with *Revolver* on one side and *Rubber Soul* on the other. It was my first deep introduction to The Beatles, really, and it was partly inspired by Ray's love of John and some of his production references. Exploring their catalogue further, I'd learned to play "Hide Your Love Away" only weeks before meeting Sean.

We passed the guitar around that night, and although we talked very little about The Beatles, I played a little bit of the opening to "Hide Your Love Away," and I'll never forget when Sean corrected me: "Actually it goes like this," assuring me, "Paul (McCartney) showed me." I passed the guitar, and Sean performed a good part of the song. He sounded so much like his father. This would be the closest thing to hearing John Lennon sing this song one could ever experience at that time. Both Ray and I were blown away. Sean played me a few of his own

compositions that night, and to this day I can still sing the chorus to the one about his cat who tragically fell from the window of the Dakota Hotel in New York where he lived. The melody was Beatles-brilliant. Sean was brilliant.

Ray and I had plans to record a new song of mine, "My Kind," the next day, and Sean had decided he wanted to come spend the day at the studio with us. Late afternoon, we picked up Sean and his friend Timo Ellis at their hotel. The band they were in town playing with on Monday was actually that of Sean's mother, Yoko Ono. They were both part of the recording band for her recently released album, *Rising*, which they were on tour supporting. With Sean's support, I took over the reins as producer that day in the studio. I insisted we were going to cut the track without a click, which I knew Ray and Harry were not excited about. Timo played drums and electric guitar, and Sean played acoustic guitar, bass, and organ. The day went well into the wee hours of the night, maybe even the next daybreak, and was chock full of creative magic. "My Kind" remains one of my favourite recordings from *Volume 1*.

I didn't see their show with Yoko at Lee's Palace the next day for some reason, but I remember an interview with Yoko Ono appearing in one of the street weekly magazines, where she expressed frustration with Sean for pulling a few all-nighters with a girl he met prior to their Toronto performance. Sorry, Yoko — that was me!

I can't remember at all if Sean and I kept in touch right after then. I don't remember talking on the phone with him or anything, and I certainly didn't have an email address in 1996. But somehow I knew he was back in town playing at Lee's Palace again later that spring with a new band called Cibo Matto. Ray and I were on the guest list — and I'm pretty sure meeting up was prearranged on the last trip.

Sean came out to the lobby before the show to meet us, and he was rather cold. I finally asked him if something was wrong, and he told me that he was upset because I had lied to him. Stunned, I truly had no idea what he was talking about. He asked me how old I was, and I answered eighteen. He said, "When did you turn eighteen?" I said April 27. I guess when I met him in late March, I had told him I was already eighteen years

old. I hadn't even remembered.

Well, this turned out to be a huge deal to Sean. I would actually never talk to him again, and after watching a little of the Cibo Matto show, I decided we had to leave. I was just so upset that I had let Sean down. I remember Ray consoling me that night for a long while as I had a good teenage cry. I really looked up to and respected Sean. And still do.

To this day, around January each year, I start thinking I'm my next age. As of February, I start answering how old I am with, "Well, I'm going to be," and by March I just answer the next age. It seems to be an inherent part of my thinking. My intention was never to deceive Sean, and I certainly regret that this happened.

Well, I had to brush myself off, because I had a lot going on. I was almost finished my record, was negotiating a record deal, and had my first cross-country tour to prepare for. Sandy had worked her magic to have me added as the opening slot on Burton Cummings' "Up Close and Alone" tour that summer, and I couldn't have been more excited.

HALF THE MAN

April 1996

Shakes bad thoughts out of his head
As he smokes a dead man's cigarette
Can't bring himself to get out of bed
'Cause he likes the thoughts running around in his head
In his head

And he only loves what he can see
And he only wishes he could be
Half the man that others see
To love himself and let it be

Can't quench the thirst when you don't have the answer
Can't come out first when you're not the better dancer
Take it as you will and take it as you must
But who is she to say what fills your heart with lust
With lust

And he only loves what he could be
And he only wishes he could see
Half the man and let it be
To love the self that others see

And he only loves what he can see
And he only wishes he could be
Half the man that others see
To love himself and let it be

☽○☾

HALF THE MAN

"Half the Man" was the very last song I wrote for my first record, *Volume 1*, in the spring of 1996. I had been studying guitar for a few years with Stratford based teacher, luthier, and inventor Michael McConville at that point. We had a unique relationship. Each lesson, he would show me challenging chords, harmonic structures, or fingerpicking patterns to satisfy my insatiable creative appetite. I would return to the next lesson with a new song I had written, most often inspired by the previous instruction. "Half the Man" was one of these songs, driven by a variation on Travis-picking Mike taught me. The picking sounds like the right hand is playing a double thumb pattern, but it isn't. When I set out to compose "Half the Man," I had the song "Scarborough Fair/Canticle" by Simon and Garfunkel faintly in my mind as melodic inspiration, although the song turned out nothing like it.

The opening line of "Half the Man" came to me one night after work at Hyacinth House. One of the waitresses there also worked as a candy striper at Stratford General Hospital. As we were all sat in the back room, the waitresses counting their cash outs and us junior hostesses polishing silverware, she pulled a carton of cigarettes from her oversized purse. Underaged, we asked where they came from, and she said that one of her patients at the hospital had passed away and his family said she could have them. One of the cooks entered the room and asked if he could light one up. We explained where they came from as he took a draw, and he shook his head. *Shakes bad thoughts out of his head

as he smokes a dead man's cigarette.* Probably a bit more literal than you were expecting.

I had known Ray for over a year, and throughout the recording process my affection for him had grown deep. Ray was passionate yet unemotional. He was simple yet routinely particular; in fact, his nickname was "Five Star." He loved dining out and drinking red wine. He cared a lot for his used BMW and maybe worked a little too hard always to project a successful image. "Half the Man" was essentially about an inner side of Ray I thought he was neglecting at the time but was certainly there. I thought the world of him despite his surface armour.

I really loved how Ray produced "Half the Man." His minimal production features a synthesized sitar playing a randomly timed, meandering drone over one chord. It's actually almost an exact recreation of The Beatles "Within You, Without You" introduction played backward. I sing all the layered harmonies, and in the bridge part where I'm scatting, the three-part harmony scoops up at the end in a long, Joni Mitchell-style blues note. When Ray suggested I sing it "like Joni," I didn't know what he was talking about. He introduced me to her album *Court and Spark*, and I never looked back. I love Joni, and that record is one of my "desert island" picks.

In the summer of 1996, through Sandy's connections, I was invited to open Burton Cummings' "Up Close and Alone" tour. I would play a twenty-to-thirty-minute solo set on my guitar, followed by Burton performing over an hour of his classics on solo piano. There was one stipulation: I had to count in and count out Burton's merchandise to the venue each night. I had to pay my own flights, and some hotels, but with a small record advance in my pocket from recently signing a deal memo with EMI Music Canada, I was ready to go.

I was a funny, determined kid. For Christmas in grade seven I'd insisted to my parents that the only thing in the world I needed was a set of matching luggage from the Samsonite outlet store in our town. I was overjoyed to find them under the tree that year, but how hilarious looking back, since I had nowhere to go with them at the time. Five years later, I packed up those suitcases and boarded a plane to meet Burton and crew in Charlottetown, P.E.I, for our first show on July 1, 1996. We wouldn't

stop until we hit Victoria, B.C. There would be five of us on the road plus our tour bus driver, the charming Charles McPhail.

Sam Boyd had the toughest job as our road manager, coordinating and wrangling all of us. Sam should be the one writing a book. Alfonz Micallef was our lighting designer, and Mick Schmidtmeyer was our soundman. Mick and Alfonz were best friends. They were both tall and lanky and had long noses. If they were cartoon characters, they would be spy vs. spy. Mick had a cool shaggy mullet and Alfonz shoulder-length black hair. They were inseparable on and off the road, where they shared a love for fixing up old hot rods. Everywhere we went, Mick and Alfonz would make sure we got up early to see the sights and show me all the important stuff. They woke me up for my first glimpse of the Rocky Mountains from the tour bus window, even though it was dark out.

It was a really unique tour experience, I would find out soon enough. Since I didn't have a record out yet, there were no in-stores to play, radio stations to visit, or interviews to do. Just free time. We'd always head to the venue mid-afternoon to do soundcheck and get the stage and merch set up. Alfonz would drape the stage with mounds of beautiful white fabric and position the lights. I would connect with the venue manager and hand off Burton's merchandise. I would often sit at Burton's piano afterward and play for Mick to get sounds. I remember once I was sounding out "These Eyes" on his piano when Burton walked onstage. "Almost," he said. "Try it like this," as he proceeded to teach me the classic piano riff. Burton would offer me tidbits of great advice: "Dayna, you want to make it in the music biz? You gotta write a song like this," and would proceed to play "Strawberry Fields Forever."

I watched Burton play every night on that tour except one, at a club called Sweetwaters in New Brunswick, where the promoter, shocked by my young age, insisted I spend the night in a locked office, except when I was performing. Burton played the same set every night and told almost the same jokes. There were a handful of diehard Burton fans who followed us across the country that summer, and I always wondered if they tired of hearing the same banter every night, until I stood beside a

few of them in the audience. They would say his punchlines before he did and were thrilled to feel a part of his inner circle. I learned a lot about putting a great show together right then and there.

I memorized all of the lyrics to Burton's famous songs from hearing him play them over and over. I had never heard "Break It to Them Gently," "Stand Tall," "Laughing," or even "These Eyes" before that tour, and I am forever grateful that I absorbed their intricate details from his live performances. Burton would buy me random little gifts from time to time to say thanks for being there. One was a beautiful little crystal dove, and then there were the lucky rocks.

Burton had these lucky rocks, you see. He couldn't go on stage without them, which I only found out about when he lost them one night in Penticton, B.C. I'll never forget a panicked Sam Boyd gathering Mick, Alfonz, Charles, and me to tear apart that bus. The show would not go on until the rocks were found!

We pretty much looked everywhere. There was a queen bedroom at the back of the bus, which no one slept in and was used more as a dressing room. It was a luxurious six-bunk bus, as opposed to the usual crowded twelve-bunk versions. Burton didn't feel safe sleeping in the back bedroom, so he took a bunk too. They had actually offered it to me at one point, but I shared Burton's logic. The rule is you sleep with your feet to the front of the bus. I was the one to finally find the rocks, tucked in the mattress of his bunk between the cushion and the wall. Adrenaline pumping, I headed to the stage to play my set and get the show started. A few days later, Burton delivered a special black velvet pouch lined with purple silk to me at soundcheck. Inside were four beautiful complimentary rocks hand-picked for me "by an Irishman," as he put it. Yes, they're in my guitar case at this very moment.

Burton really took pride in being able to afford me this opportunity. It really was the tour of all tours. We stayed in the most gorgeous hotels and played the most beautiful venues. One night, I remember being on the balcony of the Wall Centre Hotel in Vancouver. The six of us were playing a game of cards, and we all stepped outside for some fresh air. The balcony looked down over a rundown motel across the street. "Dayna," he said with pride, "That's where I stayed when I was eighteen and came to Vancouver for the first time. Look where you're staying."

What a way to see my country for the very first time. No tour ever compared for me. It must have been crazy for those guys to have an eighteen-year-old girl tagging along, but they were all perfect gentlemen, and we have all shared a special bond since. I am so grateful to Burton and crew for believing in me at such a young age, showing me the ropes and my beautiful country.

☽ ○ ☾

I'll never forget hearing myself on the radio for the first time. *Volume 1* was scheduled to be released in Canada on April 15, 1997, and "Half the Man" went to radio a few weeks earlier. Months earlier, I had moved to Toronto and shared a dark basement apartment behind a candy store called Sugar Mountain in the Beaches area of Toronto with sound engineer Annelise Noronha. My CD was in our stereo, and from time to time we would listen to it. "Half the Man" was the first song on the record, so when I wandered into the living room one morning and the track was playing, I assumed Annelise had thrown the record on while she was making coffee. But suddenly a radio DJ came on: "And that was a new song called 'Half the Man' from a Stratford, Ontario, singer-songwriter, Dayna Manning." Annelise was listening to the station Mix 99, and my eyes welled up. This wasn't my secret little project any more. Within a few weeks, "Half the Man" had made the station's top 10 list and was hitting airwaves across Canada. I was pretty proud to have a single on a top-40 radio station that didn't have drums on it in the nineties and felt that in itself was a great accomplishment.

A music video for "Half the Man" was filmed in California at a mansion in the Hollywood Hills and an abandoned building a few hours away in Joshua Tree National Park. Director George Dougherty's concept of two sides to one man was based on the character in *The Great Gatsby*, whom he instinctively felt thematically paralleled the character in "Half the Man." How true. I remember that the shooting of this video was when I had my first disagreement with EMI. They had an entire wardrobe of clothes set out for me to wear, which I was having none of. I just wanted to wear my own clothes and be myself in the video, and that's what I did.

The publicity wheel was turning, and my schedule became relentless. My days would be jam-packed with radio station visits, industry lunches, and interviews, and my schedule was detailed into fifteen-minute intervals from 8:30 a.m. to 6:30 p.m., often with a show at night.

My big Toronto live debut was on July 2nd, when I was asked to open for Radiohead at the Opera House. They were doing preview dates for their *OK Computer* album, and the musical powers that be had me added to the show. What a crazy experience. They were one of my favourite bands, and I was too frightened even to look at them at soundcheck. All my friends back home were so excited, and I remember sneaking two of them in the side door of the club to see the show. The place was packed, and it was a real test of my nerves. I don't really even remember performing, but it sure was amazing to hear iconic Radiohead songs like "Paranoid Android" and "Karma Police" live for the very first time.

That summer, I was invited to be a part of the debut year of Sarah McLachlan's groundbreaking all-female festival, Lilith Fair. Sarah's album, *Fumbling Towards Ecstasy*, was a favourite of mine, and I accepted the offer as a tremendous honour. I would join the tour with my full band for seven dates, all of the Canadian shows, and two of the shows in the northern US. The first tour date was August 15, Lilith Fair Toronto at the Molson Amphitheatre. I was so nervous that day that I actually forgot to bring my guitar and had to borrow one from my close friend Kid Carson, who was providing local backline for the show. Plagued by rainstorms, the second stage I was scheduled on was rained out, and I was bumped to play a shorter set on the main stage.

I had attended several concerts at the Amphitheatre prior to that. Through Sandy or my agent, I could usually sneak into shows, often alone, where I would always take a blanket and sprawl out on the upper lawn section of the venue. I loved watching bands with a beautiful view of the Toronto skyline behind. I could hardly believe I was about to take the stage myself.

The sound of the crowd clapping and cheering as I walked out took my breath away. It was unforgettable. It's one thing to be part of a cheering crowd that big and another to hear it from the stage. As I plugged in and found my comfort zone, I welled up with tears of gratitude. I couldn't help but take a moment to get composed. We were asked to pare the band down for this performance, so guitarist Mike Borkosky and cellist Kevin Fox joined me as an impromptu trio, and we kicked off the set with "Half the Man" and ended with "A Walk on the Moon." I sold four hundred records that day at the merch tent. Unbelievable in hindsight, considering major acts can barely sell a thousand total these days.

The Lilith dates were pretty amazing. I had lunch with the Indigo Girls one day and shared microphones with the likes of Jewel and Sheryl Crow when we all sang the Indigo Girls' hit "Closer to Fine" as the closing group number each night. I remember Burton calling me and teasing me that I was too fancy now for his tour, but the truth was that I longed for how low-key my commitments were on his tour and enjoyed it more.

The only one real hiccup on the tour was our American bus driver, who ironically for Lilith Fair, had a hard time respecting women. With Sandy in charge as our road manager, it got a little tense at times. The final straw was when we almost didn't get over the border back into Canada after the show in Minneapolis because of his past weapons charge. We asked the tour bus company to send a new driver as soon as they could. In Vancouver we picked up John, who was a total sweetheart and often drove for Vince Gill.

The bus dropped me home in Toronto after that tour on August 31st. I'll never forget it, because the first thing I learned after walking in the door was that Princess Diana had been killed in a terrible car crash fuelled by a paparazzi chase. I was so tired, but I remember sitting on the couch at home feeling a deep sadness for this senseless loss for her family and admirers.

In September I continued on the press circuit, this time throughout the United States, as Terry McBride and Nettwerk Records picked up *Volume 1* for the territory and released it on August 26th. It was a crazy schedule that had me flying to a different city every night.

In October and November, I made several live appearances on Canadian television, including *The Mike Bullard Show*, TVO's *Studio 2*, *The Pamela Warren Show*, *Canada AM*, *The Dini Petty Show*, and a short-lived variety show on CBC called the *9 O'clock Show*. It was there I met the legendary West Coast folk-rock band Spirit of the West. The show's lovely musical producer, Danny Greenspoon, had arranged to have Spirit and I perform their song "Venice Is Sinking" together to end the show.

The whole band, but especially drummer Vince Ditrich, has an insatiable sense of humour, which I couldn't help but provoke. The show prep and filming happened over two days at the CBC building at Front and John streets in Toronto. We had access to their overwhelming wardrobe warehouse and had tremendous fun picking out outfits and goofing off. Those two days and the performance were enough time to figure out that we were a good match. SOTW invited me to open their upcoming tour from Winnipeg to Victoria.

To keep things simple and cost-effective, I decided to do the shows as a duo—Kevin Fox and myself. We really were good friends, and I felt safe wandering the country with this tall, kind, talented cellist. The plan was to fly to Winnipeg, rent a car, and follow the SOTW tour bus from city to city. We didn't have credit cards, so everything was prearranged by my management in Toronto, and we showed up at the rental car company in Winnipeg but were refused the car without the credit card in hand. We tried everything. Different companies, getting the record label involved, but nothing worked.

After figuring out that buses and trains would not get us to the next gig in time, we shamefacedly approached the Spirit of the West road manager, Lance Very, and told him our dilemma. He took the scenario back to the SOTW guys, and with only one spare bunk, they allowed me to take the couch and tall Kevin to use the bunk. We travelled with them on their bus for the whole tour, bless their hearts. More than they bargained for, for sure, but they never made us feel unwelcome or like we had inconvenienced them in any way.

Vince would constantly prank Kevin and I while we were performing. Once, while Kevin and I were playing a pretty low-key ballad, the audience started laughing, and although I couldn't figure out why, I continued on.

About a minute later, I felt a large bang on the stool I was sitting on and glanced behind to see Vince, now dressed in a full-blown janitor coverall, cleaning the stage with a wide dust mop. Another night, he arrived mid-song to feed Kevin tiny powdered doughnuts as he bowed the cello. The white powder covered Kevin's face and cello, and Vince kindly returned with a napkin once the song was over. Hilarious!

Each night, I would join John Mann up front to sing "Venice Is Sinking," and at the end of each show, it was my job to run a beer on stage in the middle of their cult classic "Home for a Rest." Vince would leave the drum kit to down the bubbly brew in one go. On the last night, I had planned to get him back for all of his pranks and fill the beer bottle with Buckley's Cough Syrup, but as funny as I thought that would be, I couldn't do it. Vince and the band were just too good to me.

Spirit of the West is one of my favourite bands on the planet. They heavily influenced my work with Trent Severn and inspired my own embrace of traditional sounds in contemporary songwriting production.

My heart has broken time and again as I've followed the health battles of John Mann over the past decade. After recovering from a battle with cancer in 2011, in 2014 the band announced that John was diagnosed with early-onset Alzheimer's. An entire country of musicians and fans have rallied behind them, raising funds for specialized treatments for John and research for Alzheimer's. I was part of the 2019 "Spirit of John" fundraiser concert in Toronto, where I sang again with SOTW, minus one. It was incredible to be reunited with the band two decades later, but also incredibly sad. This was the first "Spirit of John" fundraiser John himself could not attend. John's amazing wife Jill gave a heartfelt speech mid-show, and the crowd of over eight hundred raised just shy of $120,000 for the Alzheimer Society Music Project that night.

Backstage, Jill shared that John was now living in a care facility, not too far from their home. She said he rarely spoke any more, but just days before his caregiver told him that Spirit of the West was heading to Toronto to do a fundraising concert for Alzheimer's, and he replied with "That's good." The only words he said for weeks. It was good, John, and my gosh, you were missed.

☽ ○ ☾

Volume 1 earned a Juno nomination for Best New Artist of 1998. My mother and Uncle Jerry joined me at the awards in Vancouver. This was my mother's very first time on an airplane, and I was really proud to bring her on this adventure that was beyond our wildest dreams.

David Foster was inducted into the Junos Hall of Fame that year. At the award show afterparty, he approached me, asking if I had written the song "Half the Man." I told him I wrote all of *Volume 1* myself, and he replied, "Good on ya, kid, keep up the good work."

So that was pretty cool. But having my mom there was the coolest.

MIRACLE

Cowritten with Eric Bazilian

February 2000

I've got no shame to save or lose
For now there is no wrong and there's no right
And I don't give a damn what tomorrow will bring
'Cause I'm working on a miracle tonight

The longest train, the slowest ride
Whatever gets you to the dance on time
And I might change my tune but you'll never change my mind
'Cause I'm working on a miracle tonight
I'm just working on my miracle

We all find our own way any way that we can
Just by working on a miracle
So I'm working on my miracle
We all need a little miracle

MIRACLE

"Miracle" was the first single from my second record, *Shades*. The album title name was inspired by my relationship with synaesthesia, something I discovered was unique while driving years later in Northern B.C. listening to CBC Radio. There was an hour-long feature on the phenomenon, in which one sense can perceive another that isn't there, and that was the first time I had ever heard about it. I associate colour with things that may not have colour. I have synaesthesia with music (particularly music I create), people's names, days of the week, months, letters, and numbers. I honestly thought it all came from the magnetic fridge letters I played with as a child. The album had a certain colour-tone depth to the writing for me, which I felt suited the album title. The song "Miracle" was a night sky full of navy and purple hues, with a flash of the Milky Way flowing though it.

Shades was a whole new adventure. Another world, really. In 1999, Ray and I parted ways, professionally and personally. We became too close, our relationship became complicated, and that's really the sum of it. We remain friends, and when I look back, the good memories prevail, but I know we had some pretty rough times.

Terry McBride from Nettwerk Management came on board as my manager, and my point person was a woman named Colleen Novak. I moved back to Stratford into my own apartment, EMI funded some basic recording gear, and I started writing and demoing songs for *Shades*.

Nettwerk brought a lot of consistency and normalcy to my life at the time, for which I was thankful. I think in all of 1997 and 1998 I was only home for maybe two weeks at a time. Any monies I earned would be managed in a fund I was paid a small monthly fee out of, and I even had a health care package under them. It was excellent. They gave me my first laptop computer and email address, introducing me to online communication. I remember not even knowing how to open a web browser on the blue and white MacBook when I first turned it on.

EMI was determined that I would do some cowriting for this album, unlike *Volume 1*. Let's just say I was not a fan of that in any way. Everything I had ever written was from an organic experience, and I went to a very private place to write my songs. Preplanning organic connections didn't work for me then, and it honestly still doesn't. I just couldn't envision meeting someone for coffee once and then heading back to their place to write a "masterpiece," in the sense that I hold one dear. Songwriting is more like painting to me, and I can't imagine having to negotiate painting a picture with someone else. Even in my band Trent Severn, we have never actually sat down and written a song together in a room, and we know each other pretty well. For me, songwriting is a solitary, meditative, deeply personal journey. I certainly viewed cowriting as a compromise of vision for myself as an artist.

I approached this time in my life with a closed-door attitude, which in hindsight was really too bad. I missed out on some amazing people, potential friendships, and professional opportunities. I was sent everywhere. I spent weeks meeting writers in L.A., Nashville, New York, but I just wasn't open to the connections that needed to happen. The days were filled with awkward lunches and terribly uncomfortable writing attempts with people I didn't know. Of course, I still thought they were brilliant and wonderful. I just looked at the music business for many years like the lottery. I don't think most folks can plan a big hit, or repeat one for that matter. Since it was a roll of the dice, I would rather simply stick to my vision and have a body of work I was happy with instead of chasing some parallel reality.

In the weeks I spent meeting writers while staying at LeParc Suite Hotel, a hidden oasis that looks like an apartment building on a mostly

residential street in West Hollywood, I would make only one connection that truly moved me, and that was with producer, bassist, and ex-husband of Joni Mitchell, Larry Klein. Larry was so interesting. He spoke very slowly and intentionally. I even confronted him about his communication style and remember that he explained that he thought through everything he said before he spoke it. I wasn't there, but I enjoyed his depth, perspective, and patience with life. I met with Larry several times. I spent the day at a studio once as he was producing and visited his beautiful home in Venice Beach, which had paintings by Joni herself on the wall. We would go for walks, talk about life, and he would buy me books I still hold on to. We became friends, and I cherished his outlook on life. Larry taught me a few of Joni's guitar tunings, my favourite being a version of DADGAD where the 4th string D was tuned a whole step up to an E to make DAEF#AD. He showed me some guitar patterns in this tuning that he had written. I wrote them into a song called "Go Green," which has been recorded a few times but never released.

Back in Ontario, EMI had one more meeting they wanted me to take. Near the end of this corporate process, I flew to Pennsylvania to meet a writer named Eric Bazilian. Eric has enjoyed a long, successful music career internationally since the 1980s with his band The Hooters. The band was named after the nickname for the melodica instrument, not the sleazy American restaurant chain, an unfortunate coincidence. In 1996, Eric had been nominated for songwriter of the year at the Grammy Awards for penning Joan Osborne's hit "(What if God Was) One of Us." He was quite upset that he lost to Seal's "Kiss From a Rose," and I almost understood why.

I arrived in Philadelphia with a pretty bad attitude, since these blind writing dates made me uncomfortable, and I was longing for more time on my own to write. The half-hour drive to Wayne, PA, made me soften my approach a little, as the town turned out to be fairly quaint, even a bit Stratford-like. It was on the Pennsylvania railroad and had a historic American charm.

I headed over to Eric's place midmorning the next day. He was a pretty awesome person, there were no airs about him, and although my skep-

ticism certainly took more than a day to wear off, I warmed up to him quickly. His Swedish wife Sarah was lovely, but I didn't talk with her too much, since she was very busy with their young son, and I remember that Eric had an older daughter from another marriage too. I think we enjoyed some coffee and fruit in the kitchen with his family and then quickly headed to the backyard, where Eric had converted a shed about the size of a normal bedroom into a studio. I liked the space. It wasn't fancy and felt organic. It also wasn't quite the norm back then. Most folks I had met with didn't have a home studio. Digital audio workstations were only beginning to become accessible at the time.

As we got to know each other, we bonded over a love of fingerpicking and folk music instruments and tunes. I had been messing around with the opening riff that would end up becoming "Miracle" for quite some time at that point, and he loved it. He had a lyric, "Working on a Miracle," that was nagging to be written, and the two seemed to be a perfect match.

We worked on this song for a few days. Musically, it came together pretty easily, but lyrically I struggled to cowrite. Eric pretty much let me take the lyrical reins once structure was together, and I was channelling the hard time I was having trying to find my way in the music biz, yet also trying to reflect the simple joys in life that make getting up each day worthwhile. Something Eric and his family were constantly reminding me of: family, love.

It was great to be in his studio so we could start demoing it right away. After we cut the acoustic guitars, he pulled out an electric and we started working on the guitar riff. At some point I played the opening vocal melody of Joni Mitchell's song "Clouds" over the "Miracle" fingerpicking, and it sounded awesome. Like "Half the Man," I suggested we reverse the melody, and after altering it a bit, that became most of the riff of the song. We were efficient, and despite at first seeming like mismatched socks, we found a way to fall in step and left with a fond admiration for each other.

I asked him what it was like to write "One of Us" and be a part of that experience, and he said he was simply trying to impress his wife and explain what he did for a living when he came up with the song. He had the baritone pop voice of Crash Test Dummies frontman Brad Roberts in mind when he wrote it. He even had a recording of Brad singing the song, which he played for me and I'll never forget. That was how that song was meant to be. Imagine it — it's wonderful. I was always fascinated by that song. I'm not religious, but the visuals and simplicity of the writing made me pause and reflect, as it did millions of others.

We ended up writing another song together called "Springtime," which I had started one morning at the Wayne Hotel and brought to our session. Returning to Toronto with these two new songs in hand seemed to satisfy my A&R team, and we set out to find the record's producer.

I tried recording a few of my songs with a popular Toronto-based producer, who, when we decided it wasn't working, kept all of my instruments for ransom at his studio until EMI paid their bill up to date. I was never mad about that — I'm sure he had his reasons, and I know they weren't personal, but this behaviour was par for the course in the music business, I found. I've even had to pull my own "Music Mafia Moves," as I affectionately call them from time to time.

I also recorded a few tracks at A&M Studios in L.A. with fellow EMI Music Canada artist and Tea Party frontman Jeff Martin at the production helm, along with the kind, thoughtful, and straight-laced Tea Party drummer Jeff Burrows. I really liked those recordings, although they were never released. Martin's relationship with his wife was rather tumultuous at the time, and it disturbed the recording sessions on an almost hourly basis. I think I shut this scene down pretty quickly, despite being quite pleased with the results.

I finally begged EMI to attempt to set up a meeting with a man named Jim Scott in L.A. Jim engineered Tom Petty's *Wildflowers*, and I had been worshipping him from afar for a few years at that point. They sent him *Volume 1* and the piles of demos I had been recording, and he graciously agreed to a meeting. I flew to L.A. with one of my A&R reps from EMI, Fraser Hill. My nerves were high because I had dreamed and waited for this moment for a long time and really wanted this meeting to go well.

I remember meeting Jim out on the large porch of my hotel room, either on Sunset or Hollywood Boulevard. I actually think it was at the Mondrian again, but I cannot say for sure. I can remember the view looking southwest toward the ocean behind Jim as we spoke. Jim was beyond what I had hoped. His energy was relaxed, open, and kind. I would describe him as a Californian, hippy-ish family man. I adored him instantly. He had medium-length Californian grey hair, and his smile was absolutely contagious.

Jim was very well versed in the demos I had sent and quite excited about "Miracle." And all I could think was that he was my "Miracle" in all this. I felt destined to meet Jim, and we started making plans.

DOOR 24

Summer 2000

She went away for quite some time
When she came back things were gonna be fine
There was a new look in her eye
She looked at him, began to cry

She said you don't feel right no more
I'm a slower girl than I was before
Baby you don't feel right no more
And she walked out, shut that door

She went away for a while
She came back, with that same smile
But there were new things on her mind
She'll tell you about them sometime

She said you don't feel right no more
I'm a slower girl than I was before
Baby you don't feel right no more
And she walked out, shut that door

Maybe she is, maybe she is
Right out of her mind, right out of her mind
Maybe there are, maybe there are
Things she's got to find, things she's got to find
Maybe she is running right out of time

She said you don't feel right no more
I'm a slower girl than I was before
Baby you don't feel right no more
And she walked out, shut that door
Yeah, she walked out, looking for more

DOOR 24

A song about moving on.

I arrived in California fresh in the new year of 2001 to start recording *Shades* with producer and engineer Jim Scott. I was very excited about this opportunity of a lifetime and had taken things very seriously in the months leading up to my departure. I'd purchased a gym membership for the first time and started working out on a regular basis. I spent hours each day playing the songs we were planning to record with a metronome, honing my guitar and piano chops.

Recording to me felt like an entirely different skill than performing live. One, I had to track my guitars and vocal separately, and this was difficult since I felt the combination was a delicate dance where one move dictated the next. Also, it's extremely hard to get a sense of what you sound like when you're trapped in headphones. I affectionately refer to recording as playing in the submarine, comparing the click track in the headphones to the beep of sonar, bouncing off our fingertips. In hindsight, I wished that I had a mentor who taught me the recording ropes early on, just like I had for my musical chops.

On my first record, I was a teen with no experience playing with a click track in headphones, and frankly, I couldn't cut it. Even though I wrote all the guitar parts and performed live regularly, I couldn't execute performing them perfectly in time, and we often had to hire a guitarist to learn my parts to stay on schedule. I found that pretty embarrassing, and there

was absolutely no way I would let it happen again. Especially now that I would be playing with some of my musical heroes.

Jim hired his favourite players for *Shades*. There would be five of us as the core band. We had a veteran rhythm section between Bob Glaub on bass (CSNY, Jackson Browne, Linda Ronstadt) and Don Huffington on drums (Bob Dylan, The Jayhawks, Lucinda Williams). Then up-and-comers John Ginty and Neal Casal would hold down keys and electric guitars respectively. I really looked up to John and Neal; they were only a few years older than me but were such wonderful people and musicians. It was very inspiring to spend so much time playing and learning from such graceful experts.

We spent the first week in a rehearsal hall in Hollywood, where we jammed the songs each day, working out parts, turnarounds, and arrangements. This was actually one of the first times I was able to work out my songs with a live band before recording and would be the first time I could cut bed tracks (meaning the basics of bass, drums, and rhythm instruments) with a full band all playing at the same time. I think this is a very important part of making a good record. There is a certain amount of telepathy that musicians share and develop over time, and I am certain it is audible on records, and being in headphones doesn't allow us to connect this intangible skill as well. On my first record, I had to decide on all arrangement ideas beforehand, since we recorded each part separately in a relatively small studio intended for overdubs. I sure loved the luxury that preparation, time, and space gave us. The joys of a major-label budget.

We would spend the next two months recording at Cello Studio, 6000 Sunset Boulevard, right beneath the iconic Hollywood sign. Cello was renamed in 1999 but was originally known as the smaller building of the United Western Recorders, founded in 1961, and later became Ocean Way in the early 1980s. An unbelievably long list of incredible records has been recorded there.

There were three studios housed at 6000 Sunset. Studio 1 was an orchestra room famous for recording many of Frank Sinatra's hits live off the floor. Its angled white walls almost had a school gym feel, and

it is the biggest recording studio I've ever been inside. Studio 2 was a large, rectangular room with high ceilings covered in wooden slats, with a few isolation booths used to separate singers and amps from the rest of the band so that unwanted sound didn't bleed into microphones. I remembered seeing photos of Studio 2 on the album jacket of Tom Petty's *Wildflowers*. Many famous rock bands have cut Grammy-winning records in this room, including a few while I was there. The third studio was possibly the most famous room, more of an overdub room, where Brian Wilson recorded *Pet Sounds* and The Mama and Papas recorded the likes of "California Dreamin'." By the time I finished *Shades* I would have the honour of recording in all three studios. Cello felt like my mecca, and I couldn't believe at just twenty-two years old, I was working there.

The building was a rectangle, with the shorter side facing the street. If you walked in the front door you would be greeted by reception. You could then turn right and would have to make a quick left down the longest corridor in the building. On the left-hand side of this corridor were lounges that coordinated with each studio, where artists and musicians could relax when they weren't needed in the sessions. Studio 1 was on the left, Studio 3 on the right, and Studio 2 was across the whole back end of the building.

We would start recording in Studio 2 to cut our beds. I arrived the first day to a musical wonderland. Jim had a certain aesthetic and travelled with tapestries, Oriental rugs, Christmas lights, flashing signs, and pictures. The walls of the entire control room were covered in tapestries layered with coloured string lights, topped off with velvet portraits of Elvis and Willie Nelson. The tracking floor was jammed with instruments. The right was a lineup of keyboards, starting with a variety of organs, and ended with a grand piano. A smaller room toward the back housed a variety of guitar amps, where Neal Casal would anchor his guitar station. To his right was Bob's bass station, and Don's drum riser was on the right side of the room in front of Bob. I would spend my time in the vocal booth in the front right corner of the room. Coloured lights and tapestries made their way in anywhere Jim could put them. Hanging at the back of the tracking room was a huge light-up sign surrounded in flashing raw lightbulbs with changeable plastic letters. It said *Welcome Dayna

Manning*, which honestly made me grin pretty hard that first day. We would change the letters to celebrate birthdays and inspire as needed.

We worked on two-inch tape. Loads of two-inch tape. At the speed we were working at, each tape could record about fifteen minutes of twenty-four-track music. Each track had a different instrument recorded on it and coordinated to a strip on the Neve console in the control room where Jim operated all the equipment. Each strip controlled the level, sound, and EQ of each track. We must have had thirty reels of tape going, since we would do four to six takes of each song, listen back, and decide which take to move forward with. The tapes all lived on a grey cart that would get wheeled around the place like a hospital cart.

Recording with Jim was an amazing experience. Although not a musician himself, he owned the most gear of anyone I've ever known, which was kept in a nearby warehouse. I played his vintage Martin and Gibson acoustics. The organs and drum kits were all his, and when we wanted to change the snare sound, we grabbed one of the several other snare drums on hand, lined up in the hallway. The big recording secret I was looking for was right there: put a good sound in front of a good mic. Jim spent years collecting the good sounds.

We worked Monday to Saturday and took Sundays off, which I basically slept away to recharge for the next week. We kept late hours, arriving around noon or 1:00 p.m. and working past midnight most days. Jim cherished his mornings with his young kids and wife Carol, and I certainly wasn't a morning person at the time. I was actually staying up extra late every day, taking the mixes from the work we did that day on CD and driving all over Hollywood listening to them. My rented apartment was about twenty minutes away, but I'd usually drive around for an hour listening to mixes and making plans for the next day.

On one track, I think it was "Springtime," I liked the first half of one take and second of another. If it were today, this would be no problem; working in a digital audio workstation like ProTools, we would just copy and paste the different takes together as if we were working in Microsoft Word. But back then, there wasn't really a way we could combine the tracks, unless you were working with the likes of Jim. As soon as we all agreed, he just

cut the tapes and taped them together perfectly. He would fly guitar solos from one take into another. It was amazing to see in action.

A few weeks later, we moved into Studio 3 for overdubs. We were recording right where Brian Wilson had recorded one of my favourite songs, "God Only Knows." It was in this studio that I would sing most of my lead vocals, play the piano on "Like a Werewolf," and where we overdubbed percussion and more guitars. We had an opportunity to have Greg Leisz play pedal steel on a few tracks; I'd seen him play with Joni Mitchell at Maple Leaf Gardens in 1998, and I was thrilled to have him join us for the day.

Jim Scott was a popular fella. We would regularly be visited by famous guests recording next door and in the studios around us. Producer Don Was, (Tom Petty and the) Heartbreakers pianist Benmont Tench, and session drummer Kenny Aronoff would make regular appearances. Jim Keltner, one of the most legendary drummers in musical history, even popped his head in once to say hello. I was star-struck every single day.

I remember one day we were going to do some simple task like tape backups that didn't require me to be there most of the day, and Jim suggested I take the time to check out Hollywood Boulevard and see some sights. But I insisted that I would stay, saying that I'd dreamed of being there all my life and wasn't planning on missing a minute, although I was coaxed away one afternoon by Neal and visiting producer George Drakoulias to peruse vintage guitars at all the specialty shops in town. Pretty memorable.

Once, Jim and I ventured out to visit legendary producer Rick Rubin's home, just off Sunset Boulevard in the Hollywood Hills, to borrow a rare instrument called a Chamberlin organ. We were greeted by an assistant who ushered us through a large foyer with a massive Buddha at the far end into a small office. After a short visit, she told us Rick would be sad to miss us, but he was in the studio downstairs with Johnny Cash and couldn't be disturbed. Wow.

While I was recording, there were other projects happening around me. System of a Down moved into Studio 2 to record their breakthrough album, *Toxicity*. Neal Casal was producing a duet EP titled *Ran on Pure Lightning* with an artist named Shannon McNally in Jim's Lounge at Cello — a small, secret fourth room where Jim housed a very small Neve console and extra

supplies. I ended up singing backups on a song titled "Pale Moon" on that record. I'll never forget the places that song took me the first time; I fell so in love with it that I ended up recording "Pale Moon" on my next record.

Communications from EMI were sparse during my recording. I can remember one quick visit from A&R close to the end of recording, and we didn't receive any feedback. When I finally made it back to Canada in March, I was devastated to hear that EMI was not happy with the record.

They felt it was too country-sounding; I felt it was more Americana. They wanted the beautiful pedal steel off the record and quite a few changes made. I was heartbroken and took some time to go home and digest their feedback.

They wanted me to recut two tracks, "I'm the Girl" and "Door 24." While I didn't want to change them, I did want to go back to California and work with Jim again, so I agreed. I would head back in June for a few weeks. The original tracks would still be there, and I thought only good could come of it. Also, I was often motivated by the experience and not the result.

Between the time I left California and the time I returned, Jim had been engineering some demo tracks for the Red Hot Chili Peppers' next album and had played some of my stuff for drummer Chad Smith. Chad expressed admiration for my fingerpicking style and asked Jim if he could be the drummer for our next session. Of course, I jumped at the opportunity to work with one of my favourite drummers. "Door 24" is a fast fingerpicking song I wrote in the Joni tuning Larry Klein taught me, DAEF#AD, and I couldn't wait to hear what take Chad Smith would have on it.

Neal and Bob returned to the studio with Chad and I, this time in Studio 1, the only room available at Cello. I was nervous to be around Chad. I'd listened to his records a million times, learned his songs when I was a teen, and really couldn't believe this was happening. Chad was welcoming, funny, and supportive, and I just took it all in. He had an assistant/friend with him most of the time who resembled RHCP singer Anthony Kiedis to me, but perhaps a bit smaller. Chad's newborn daughter visited us in the studio, and it was lovely to just have all the good vibes of another kind human around us. Chad's playing was creative, punchy, and fantastic, and I was having the time of my life jamming away with this legend.

The studio dynamic was a bit different on this trip. Most of Rage Against the Machine had moved into Studio 2 and 3 when I got there, to work on a new project with Chris Cornell. Little did I know that Audioslave was forming beside us. I would occasionally pass Cornell in the hall and say hello, and guitarist Tom Morello once even popped his head in to borrow my capo. My inner teenager was absolutely dying every day.

The pinnacle moment was one evening in early June. I was sitting outside on a makeshift deck at the back of the guarded parking alleyway and beside the side-door entranceway to the Studio 2 hallway. It was a gorgeous Californian evening, clear and blue. All the doors to the studio were wide open, including to the tracking room floor as everyone let the breeze freshen their room and lungs. I could hear the Rage fellas getting sounds, and eventually they broke into "Kashmir" by Led Zeppelin. Almost simultaneously, several helicopters started flying overhead, headed toward downtown L.A. I had no idea what was happening, except that perhaps I was in a new Rage Against the Machine video? I really didn't know what was going on, but I'll never ever forget the moment, thinking, *No one will ever believe this*.

Later, I found out the Los Angeles Lakers and Philadelphia 76ers were battling it out in the NBA finals, and it was a regular occurrence for folks to take to the streets after these games. That's where the helicopters were headed, toward the Staples Centre downtown. It sure made for an intensely dramatic moment I would never forget, as the spinning blades blended with the absolute musical heaviness coming from beside me.

Despite all these amazing adventures and efforts, EMI still didn't like the record. They even wanted Chad Smith scrapped on one track, and I was upset. The next year was a bit of a waiting game from both sides. I was hoping they would grow to like it, and they were hoping I'd redo many more tracks. I ended up tweaking and redoing some tracks with Toronto producer Dave Hodge, who I thought did a great job, but ultimately *Shades*, released almost a year and a half later in the fall of 2002, ended up a compromise for me, and the result wasn't the record I or EMI hoped to put out. It was somewhere in the middle, which seemed mediocre to me and left our relationship in a bad place.

Somewhere in this time, EMI had decided that they would like me to join forces with fellow EMI labelmates Damhnait Doyle and Kim Stockwood to form a trio. I was good friends with Damhnait and certainly thought both artists were great talents, but it wasn't what I was interested in doing. At first EMI thought it should be a cover project and had a meeting with the three of us and a long list of peculiar covers they thought we should tackle. It was an adamant no from me, over and over. I didn't care if I was going to lose my record deal over it. Eventually they believed me and invited Tara McLean as the third, forming the trio Shaye, named after Tara's beloved sister who tragically passed away as the band was forming. I thought Tara was a great fit, being from P.E.I and both Damhnait and Kim hailing from Newfoundland; they had an East Coast core to draw from.

I did a few tours to support *Shades*. The first was a triple bill with Holly McNarland and Wide Mouth Mason. There I met Holly's bassist, Joel Meyers, who would introduce me to Matthew Good Band drummer Ian Browne, who would join me on my next tour with Remy Shand as MGB went their separate ways. I loved Ian's playing and was thrilled to be working with him. We would end up working together a lot more on my next album, *Folkyo*.

The most exciting tour was when I was invited to open a handful of shows, solo acoustic, for Joe Cocker across western Canada in the spring of 2003. I flew to Calgary on my own, rented a car, and basically found my own way to each show. I would play about a half hour, and then Joe and his band would rock the stage. We played larger venues like The Orpheum in Vancouver and Jack Singer Hall in Calgary.

Despite playing several dates with Joe and finding time to talk with most of his musicians, I never met Joe personally. He never, ever used the venue dressing rooms; his driver parked his tour bus beside the stage door, and Joe would enter and exit the stage directly from there. Joe did write me a lovely note at the end of the tour thanking me for joining him, but I sadly haven't been able to find it for years. I sure loved the opportunity to watch him every night, and honestly that was thanks enough for me. I was just so grateful to be there.

ANYTOWN

Cowritten with Gavin Bradley

Sometime in 2004

Sometimes I love this place
And sometimes I don't
Some days everything goes my way
Some days it just won't
I sit around and plan what I can do to get what I want
And I spend too much time thinking of everything I'm not
But of all the lost and found, I'm no one's hand-me-down

If you're waiting around too long,
You might find your chance is gone
Be forced to take it all in stride
'Cause it's all part of the design
Of any room
In any house
On any street
In Anytown

Half my friends are married
And half of those have kids
They love to hear my stories
Of where I've been and what I did
We all suspect each other's lives are better off
Freedom, love, success, whichever we ain't got
As street lights flash on and off, I wonder is this really where I'll end up?

If you're waiting around too long
You might find your chance is gone
Be forced to take it all in stride
'Cause it's all part of the design
Of any room
In any house
On any street
In Anytown

You try to imagine
You close your eyes
But that's all in the design
Of any room
In any house
On any street
In Anytown

ANYTOWN

As amazing as making *Shades* with Jim was experience-wise, artistically I just always wanted to be in the driver's seat and started to tinker away recording at home a lot more. As things cooled off publicly in the summer of 2003, I was still full steam ahead in my heart. Living back in Stratford, I felt active as ever and got my hands on my first version of ProTools with an MBox interface.

I was hanging around Toronto a lot with producer/writers Jon Levine and Gavin "Gavo" Bradley, and with the arrival of digital audio workstations on our personal computers, we were all starting to be able to create a bit more on our own terms for the first time. Gavo, John, and I weren't exactly working together; we were more just hanging out, keeping each other laughing all the time, and working when it made sense. We would talk shop a lot, I sang a demo for Jon, he played piano on my tunes, and I learned lots of ProTools and producer chops just by being around them. For some reason they would always make fun of me for living in Stratford, but I truly think it's just that they simply hadn't been here. It sounds like all the other small towns, but it's just not. "Anytown" was inspired by Gavo's take on imagining my small-town life in Stratford, and me looking around wondering if my life was actually going in the direction I wanted it to, and I wasn't really sure. My friends had graduated university, were starting to plan marriages and families, and I was starting to realize that although my life was jam-packed with adventure and opportunity, I was missing out on creating my own happy home. My friends wanted to know all about my life, and I wanted to know all about theirs. I was missing out on some important relationships.

Despite this awareness, I just kept plugging away at what I knew best and started writing songs for a third record. Months earlier, while in Vancouver on tour at the Commodore Ballroom, Ian Browne reintroduced me to an artist named Christian Thor Valdson, who I first met at the 1998 Juno awards. He and his band Copyright were sitting behind me then, and I remember Christian talked my ear off. Their album *Love Story* was nominated for Best Alternative album that year. Christian was an incredibly talented and unique fella. He and Ian had been working together on some instrumental tracks and decided to send a few my way, which I instantly loved and started rearranging and writing vocals to. I could import them into ProTools, chop them up, rearrange them, and then sing over the tracks.

I asked EMI to support a trip to Vancouver so we could work out some ideas, which they did happily. We rented iconic West Coast band 54-40's studio/jam space for a week, and Ian engineered the sessions. Along with Joel Meyers on bass, we recorded maybe seven or eight songs, which I then took home to my studio and worked on. I think four eventually made my next album, *Folkyo*: "Gloria," "Robot Eyes," "Tears," and "I'll Go."

I realized I was loving cowriting because I had time and space to establish natural friendships with my cowriters and time to work on the song by myself to make arrangement calls. I was never cowriting with the pressure of being in the same room. I loved finishing other people's ideas. I was really happy with the songs coming out and quite excited to move forward. I wrote more songs with Anjulie Persaud, Julian Tomarin, and Ashton Price.

I had a meeting with the head of A&R at EMI, Tim Trombley, at a Greek restaurant near the EMI offices in Mississauga. He seemed really happy with the direction I was headed in and psyched to continue. Nothing about it felt weird, and I thought we were all systems go.

I can't remember the exact details of the next few weeks, but basically

EMI had somehow changed their minds since my meeting with Tim and made the decision not to do a third record with me, and through email, they dropped me. No phone call, no nothing. It was just done. There was never another conversation about it, except when I unsuccessfully tried to buy my masters back for a dollar from Deane Cameron. I know. Pretty cheeky, but seriously.

Although folks expected me to be devastated, I really wasn't. I wasn't happy. I knew our artist/label relationship wasn't working. I never felt that my ability to write songs and share them with an audience was dependent on them, and honestly, I was barely making a living being a recording artist. In fact, I wasn't at all. I was left in a lot of debt, trying to uphold some image of a professional musician, and I wanted to be done with it, despite really adoring each individual I worked with at the company. I paid most of my bills with part-time jobs and live shows, and being a recording artist almost felt beside the point to me. Anything I did for EMI was actually costing me income at that point, since I wasn't successful enough to make any money from it. I felt that ultimately, music was in me, as it always had been, record company or no record company.

Over the next few months and years, really, I had a tough time figuring out how I was going to finish my third record. I was really lucky to have about half of it done, between the demos from Vancouver and my work. I spent a significant amount of time making plans to ask for private investors, started down that road, and got scared. And crowdfunding wasn't the norm back then like it is now. I wrote one hell of an application to the Ontario Arts Council and got funded. But I had to match the funds.

I think everyone thinks that if you were on MuchMusic in the nineties, your bank account was doing all right. But that just wasn't true. Beyond a record advance, which for me was around $50,000 per record – minus lawyer, accounting, and management fees, almost anything else I did I did not get paid for, although expenses were covered. And there was no time limit on how long the record could take to make, so in the case of *Shades*, I was living on that advance for several years, so realistically I was working full-time for them for a very small $10,000 a year. Every day I worked on the record, played a show, shot a video, I was paid a per diem — a fee of about $30 a day at the time to cover food and small expenses. So If I went to L.A. for the week, I had $210 in my pocket, which was quite all right, as long as there were no bills at home to pay. Everyone around me — producers, engineers, musicians — were being paid at their full rate, and I may have done much better simply to be paid for my work like everyone else.

Here's the basics of how my record deal, and most of them worked: The record company would send an advance my way, which would cover my commitment to recording and promoting the record. They would also pay for the entire demoing and recording of the album. One hundred percent of these costs would end up in my recoupable account, which I would pay back to the record company out of my portion of record sales before I would see any more funds from my recording. They would also provide monies for video production and tour support, since most beginner bands couldn't secure guarantees from venues high enough to cover their costs. Fifty percent of these costs would be added to my recoupable account, among other specific marketing costs. Artists received no monies when videos were played on MuchMusic. This was considered advertising. Videos were basically considered commercials for the album by the industry.

My recoupable account would be paid back to the record company from my portion of record sales, which was about ten percent. For basics, here's that calculation generously. Store sells CD for $20. Record company sold it to them for fifty percent at $10. I received ten percent of that figure, which is $1.00, which entirely goes toward my recoupable account, until it is a hundred percent paid off. If I didn't make the money, I didn't owe them it. It was a loan you only paid back if you made the money. Most artists I know from that era didn't recoup their accounts, but some were smarter than others about it, spending a lot less up-front. I honestly didn't know any better. When EMI and I parted ways, I was a significant liability, with my recoupable account close to a million bucks.

The chances I had to make money to live were through mechanical licenses — being the writer of my music. SOCAN (The Society of Composers, Authors and Music Publishers of Canada) collected royalties on radio airplay and public performances and paid us every three months. I would stand to make some money if songs were licensed though my mechanical, but any right bought to the recording would go to EMI. I made money selling merchandise and my CDs from the side of the stage, which I was allowed to buy from EMI for fifty percent of retail price, just like any other retailer. Occasionally a show would come for which I didn't need tour support, and if there was money left over, I would get a paycheque. But let me tell you, this was very rare. I pretty much held down full-time employment from late 2001 on, while managing all my commitments of touring and having a record deal.

Hindsight is 20/20, and to be honest I was likely too young to handle all the attention and responsibility that came my way with a record deal at eighteen. In recent years, I've viewed this time in my life as the equivalent to my university education, including the personal debt just to keep on living that came with it. Except that everything I learned in this school gets flipped upside down as technology progresses. Every time I make a record, I feel like I'm in a new business, one that as a businesswoman I haven't had any say in. At every turn it seems like there are completely different roadblocks and changing methods of delivery.

The streaming thing really gets to me. What gets to me the most is that the same company that has been instrumental in bringing steaming to the forefront has been the one eliminating the tools we use to digest music. Upon the introduction to the iPod, Apple slowly wiped out CD drives from its computers. With the popularity of streaming, they made it nearly impossible for anyone to manage the digital music content on their devices, fearing sync issues between iPods, iPhones, and computers would wipe out our musical library. I've stopped updating my devices, since the updates render them useless. My iPods are time capsules. This is monopoly at its finest, and as an independent artist, it's devastating to me to have absolutely no way to distribute my music on my own, since no one has a convenient way to listen to it. I truly feel forced into use streaming services to distribute my recordings.

In my house, the vinyl record rules, and it's not because we are sonic snobs. It's because we love to listen to albums, like we love to watch a movie. We were able to buy a turntable and purchase records we loved at a local shop. My CD player broke years ago, and I haven't been able to replace it. We still buy CDs for the 2002 Subaru, but I know that the next car likely won't have the option to listen to them. Without the CD drive in my computer, I can't make them into files, and adding them to my device is beyond me — yet I can produce and engineer an entire record by myself. Hmmm.

I'm certainly frustrated with this business as an artist and a consumer. But luckily, I'm not beyond frustrated with music.

☽ ○ ☾

After an unexpected winter spent in Northern British Columbia (see next chapter), I was finally able to finish my third record, *Folkyo*, with a lot of help in the spring and summer of 2006. A high school friend of mine named Siegfried Meyer, who has become a very successful producer, was on his way up back then, and we connected and struck up a deal to finish the project, piece by piece.

I had spent less than a tenth of what was spent on *Shades* and was just as happy with the results, if not more. I felt destined to be an independent artist, so I started learning skills to support this. I took a few courses on how to use Photoshop and Illustrator to start designing my own posters and art, started promoting many of my own shows, and learned more about production any chance I could. I released *Folkyo* on my own label and secured a Canadian distribution deal with Festival Distribution. Within a year that company folded, and I lost much of the product I gave them, along with any profits. The Mp3 era was here.

As it stands, I am now extremely thankful to have the career I do. Being part of the marketing machine the major labels were in the late nineties and early two thousands meant that a lot of folks interested in Canadian music know my name, and that has come with great advantages getting grants, gigs, and support. Marketing these days is such a blur, and any of us artists who were part of the era of focus are still benefiting from it.

When I wrote "Anytown," I was really questioning this whole pursuit. I often reflect that when I started making my first record, a lot of my pals were into skateboarding. None of those friends still skateboard. Should I still be pursuing music? I always end up at yes. If the songs keep coming, and I feel there is something important to document, you'll be hearing from me.

I heard a rumour I could find you at the New Frontier
I kept fixing my hair, checking my lips in the mirror
Two-step, back-step, turn around and dip your head back, cowboy
Shake those lazy hips in my direction, eternal connection
Oh Charlie, baby, sweetie, won't you dance all night

Oh Charlie, It's just you and I
And with your hand on my back, I feel your cold dark side
You've acted strange, since those twelve men drowned
But I forget all about it when you dance around

And they told me if I whistled, you would dance all night, all night
So I stayed up 'til the morning light, morning light
Yeah, they told me if I whistled, you would dance all night, all night
And so I stayed up 'til the morning light

We all knew that you were staying over in those caves
Because after you left we found your raven's grave
But when you drank our water, it got in your soul
You can run and hide, but you can't shake the hold
As time flies by, time can run you back too

Oh Charlie, look up in the sky
You're such a beautiful sight for a cold dark night
We've looked at you strange, since those twelve men drowned
But there's still love in our eyes when you dance around

And they told us if we whistled, you would dance all night, all night
And so I stayed up 'til the morning light, morning light
Yeah, they told us if I whistled, you would dance all night, all night
And so we all stayed up 'til the morning light

CHARLIE LAKE

Charlie Lake holds so much significance for me.

I actually can't recall exactly when I first heard of Charlie Lake, British Columbia, and the famous Charlie Lake Cave, where some of the earliest evidence of human activity in North America has been found. It was either in a history book, or on my first or second trip to perform in Fort St. John, British Columbia. The first trip was in February of 2005.

I received an email from my friend Jason George, a promoter from the Kitchener, Ontario area who had booked me a few times. He was now the general manager of a hotel complex in FSJ and had a decent entertainment budget. Instead of sourcing locally, since he knew no one at the time – and I think pickings were slim due to the low population – he would hire solo artists he'd worked with from back in Ontario, the likes of myself, Danny Michel, Lindy, Matt Mays, Justin Rutledge, Brian Byrne, etc. We would make the trek west and perform four days in a row from time to time. The gig came with decent pay, a hotel room, travel, and all meals covered.

Fort St. John is located at mile 47 of the Alaska Highway and is the oldest European-established settlement in modern-day British Columbia. I flew into Edmonton then took an overnight Greyhound Bus – eight hours, I believe – to get there. It was a long and interesting trip, full of colourful and sometimes sketchy characters. When I arrived, I thought I was in the middle of the prairies. This was not the stereotypical mountainous British Columbia I was used to. It looked more like Saskatoon than Revelstoke. I felt like I had no idea where I was. Soon enough, I'd learn that I was on the tip of the prairies that bursts into northern B.C. We were seventeen hours northeast of Vancouver and an hour away from the Alberta border.

I waited a few minutes at the bus depot, then Jason picked me up. I remember being very glad to see him by then and wondering what exactly I had gotten myself into. Off to the hotel we went. The place was brand new and especially nice for a Super 8. Attached were a cozy restaurant and an Irish pub called Egan's. There was a little hallway that connected the two. Some gigs feel like "tourcations," and this was certainly one of them. No press schedule, just free time, music, good people, and all the food and drink I desired.

In the pub before the first show, I met one of the waitresses named Laura, with whom I instantly hit it off. She gave me the lay of the land and explained the different folks and happenings. I remember that the town was very spread-out and hard to walk; it was kind of like trying to walk around an urban sprawl shopping suburb so I didn't venture too far, but after that first performance, I knew this town was different. The people had an ambitious energy, and little did I know, its nickname was "The Energetic City."

After the show, I remember a fella named Angus showing us magic tricks. He was a teacher and really kind. I met his friends, Peter and Sean. Sean was handsome and made me laugh, but I didn't think too much about it at the time. I even think we all went out dancing one night at a place called Backwoods where Laura taught me to two-step. I don't think much else was happening around town, so many folks seemed to return nightly, and after playing only four shows, I actually felt like I was part of the community.

Soon enough, I travelled home but kept in regular contact with Laura and Jason. I wanted to go back, so we scheduled another set of gigs there for June 2005. This trip was the first time I had experienced the late-night and early-morning sun of the north. I remember Jason saying that some nights they would leave the bar and go tee off at the golf course because the sun was already starting to rise at 3:00 a.m. The extended daylight sure felt like magic to me.

One of the nights I performed on that June trip, a waitress was serving a huge table of young men sitting close to the stage, having a good time, but not out of hand or anything. There were about nine or ten of them. Word got out that their bill came to over $900. I asked my friend Laura about this, and she said a lot of people in the town had money to burn because they were working in oil and gas "camps" outside of town for a few weeks at a time, and on days off, they came to town looking to blow off steam and enjoy themselves. I pictured MacGyver. Army tents. Not quite.

Well, my mind did the calculation on the tip for that table. As a one-time waitress in my younger days, I knew what a night at that pace would look like. My mind started turning. Quite alluring for a young, struggling artist who had just lost her record deal, trying to finish a half-done independent record.

It was on this trip that I became determined to see the Charlie Lake Cave for myself. I was absolutely fascinated and just had to visit the site. I started asking around about them between sets. Some folks had heard of them, some folks hadn't. They weren't widely publicized in the area and were actually located on private land. I spotted the nice fella, Sean, from my previous trip in February, sitting at the bar alone. I asked Laura to remind me of his name, and we started chatting.

I asked Sean about the caves. He seemed as excited about them as I was and volunteered to take me to visit them the next afternoon. He picked me up in his big white truck, and off we went, five miles up the highway to Charlie Lake. We turned off the highway to the right just before the lake and then made another quick right, where we parked on the side of the road. I realized then that if it were winter, when the trees were bare, you would have been able to see the caves right from the Alaska Highway.

The dirt road we were stopped on wound around a small hill to the left. There was a faint beaten path across the street, leading up the hill. We hiked maybe thirty feet up to the cave. Just right there, for anyone to visit, albeit illegally due to it being private property, but that didn't seem to be enforced. The cave wasn't huge and was made entirely of rock. I don't think I could quite stand up in it, but one could imagine sitting around sharing secrets with teenage friends. There was evidence some antics had happened recently. A metre-high matching rock wall stood in front of the cave, almost forming an aisle to the entrance. I remember the view taking my breath away. There were the usual trees at that latitude, lots of poplar and pines, but through them you could glimpse the Rockies in the distance over flat prairie. The mountains must have been two, maybe three hours away but were easy to see. The vantage point felt safe, historic, and perfect. We spent some time in the sun, took some photos, and admired the view. It was a very moving experience; I felt connected with the ancient past.

Back home, my third record and first independent album, *Folkyo*, was about half done, and I needed to figure out a way to fund completing it. I had a grant from the Ontario Arts Council but had to match the funds. I ran an idea by Jason. What if I came up in October, but then I stayed on as a waitress for him for a couple months? He was understaffed, and labour was hard to find in a booming oil and gas town paying $20+ for unskilled labourers. I could save up some money, explore the relationships I had formed, then head home and finish my record. Signing a record deal while still in high school doesn't make for the best backup plan.

Jason was game, so he flew me up. I played my shows and reported for training Monday morning. Friends helped me find a room to rent, and I was off and running. I was only blocks away from work, but I'll never forget the cold walks there. Minus 20 Celsius was the norm, but somehow it was all right because it was almost always sunny. I truly fell in love with the climate and still yearn for that winter sun through my current Ontario winters. Fort St. John is one of the sunniest places in British Columbia, especially in the winter and spring. The city holds the provincial record for most sunshine ever recorded in March, May, and November. This was uplifting and inspiring, despite the restricted sunlight hours in the winter. Sometimes it didn't get light out until close to 10:00 a.m. and the sun would set again by 4:00 p.m.

This crazy adventure started the next chapter of my life in motion. I returned to Ontario after that winter to complete and release *Folkyo*. But in October 2006, I would return to Fort St. John to live with Sean and start a new life. We had fallen in love, and I wanted a big change. I had fallen out of love with the music industry, despite music being my truest love. I needed to find my way back to my real relationship with music, and the north helped me with that in many ways.

Sean and I had a few lovely years together, but in 2009 our breakup was abrupt, and so dramatic and heart-wrenching for me that I sometimes find it hard to remember the good times. On my own again and thousands of miles from my family, I went through a slew of jobs, my favourite working at a design and media firm called Motion Media, and the longest making technical diagrams for a company called Cenergy. I was very grateful for these opportunities, which helped get me back on my feet and ultimately home to Stratford.

It was during my time at Cenergy that I met John and Patricia Sagert. John was a coworker who had the best sense of humour. His energy reminded me of Beaker from *The Muppet Show*, and his dry humour often made me feel like I was on an episode of *The Office*. This takes us to September 9, 2011.

That night, John invited us all to their place for a BBQ. He and Patricia live on the north side of Charlie Lake in a home that used to be a float-plane pilot hotel, a place to stop for the night and dock a bush plane. This converted treasure was right on the water and had a huge deck where we all enjoyed dining and conversing. They asked me to bring my guitar, and as the sun went down and the stars came out, I was singing away. Then, suddenly, the Northern Lights appeared. This particular show was spectacular, rainbow colours dancing in the sky. We would see the lights relatively often up there, but this display was much more vivid than usual and was only enhanced as the auroras reflected off Charlie Lake.

That night I was taught that if you whistled at the Northern Lights, they would dance. I took note of the spooky intervals folks chose to whistle at the phenomena. I had to be somewhere bright and early, so after enjoying the lights for more than an hour, I headed back to my house in FSJ.

I distinctly remember this drive because folks were unusually outside at this hour, gazing at the sky, talking to their neighbours, attempting to take pictures of the dancing lights. I loved how they united people in beauty and awe.

The next day, I made a post on social media about it. *Last night I sang under the Northern Lights, the moon and the stars, on a dock with a cat, on Charlie Lake. It is now a precious memory. A big thanks to the Sagerts.*

A friend commented, *You have GOT to write a song about THAT!* And my wheels started turning.

I had always wanted to write a song about Charlie Lake, ever since I felt that "I'm a tiny speck of dust in the universe, yet we are connected to everything" feeling when I visited the caves for the first time more than six years earlier.

I started to contemplate my feelings for the area, the history I knew, and to dig deeper. I found information online though the Simon Fraser University website. The university undertook excavations of the site twice, the earliest led by archaeologist Knut Fladmark in 1983.

I read about how they found fluted points and other artifacts, along with animal remains close to 11,000 years old. Two ravens found there are believed to be some of the first signs of spirituality or ritual in Canada because of the way they were buried. How amazing to be a neighbour to this cave.

The Charlie Lake Monument also stood out in my mind. Erected while I was living in the area in 2008, it commemorates the lives of twelve men who drowned in Charlie Lake on May 14, 1942, while the U.S. Army was building the Alaska Highway.

According to the historical sign that accompanies the stainless steel monument, seventeen men had set out on a large makeshift pontoon with supplies and equipment in the early morning. The water was choppy, with one-foot waves. Late morning, as the waves grew, a flaw was discovered in the raft and it was ordered ashore. A local trapper named Gustaf Albin Hedin, who had been watching the pontoon make its way down the lake while cooking breakfast in his north shore cabin, suddenly noticed the raft was nowhere to be found. It's said that the pieced-together vessel sank in under two minutes after waves flooded the right pontoon as the vessel turned on a precarious angle. Hedin could see its crew struggling in the water and set out fifteen minutes away in his fourteen-foot rowboat. Despite two-to-three-foot waves at that point, he was able to rescue five men in three trips.

The steel monument stands twelve feet high in a twelve-foot circle surrounded by twelve posts, one for each of the soldiers who drowned that day. The monument is a must-see when studying the highway and history of the area. It's located at the mouth of Charlie Lake, with small, rolling hills on either side of the lake framing it in the distance.

There were lots of other local tales and stories I wanted to include in my song. Everyone in the area was always telling me that if I drank the water, my soul would return. I would hear this story a lot, probably because of the unlikely circumstance of me ending up there for so many years.

I also loved the phrase "Let's run him off" that I would hear oil and gas workers use for someone who wasn't pulling their weight in the field. I pictured a lonely man running down the Alaska Highway in the standard fireproof coveralls used in the area.

The first line of the song, "I heard a rumour I could find you at the New Frontier," was inspired by a country dance saloon my friends and I would frequent. Country music and two-stepping was the dance of the area and I became quite good at it over the years. The place to go in 2011 was called The New Frontier. You could find me there with my girlfriends once a week, waiting for friends and mysterious cowboys to ask us for a dance. It wasn't necessarily a courting ritual; it was a skill, and frankly, I loved working on my two-stepping twists, turns, and tricks. I really miss this part of the culture now, living back in Ontario.

While writing the song "Charlie Lake," I pictured how we would all get dressed up, running to the bathroom in between dances with my best friends Shannon, Randelle, and Marie to check our lip gloss and make sure our hair was intact. It was all so fun and nostalgic to me.

When I sing "Charlie Lake," I picture a certain fella, a very fit, large man with a black cowboy hat we all loved to dance with. I don't remem-

ber his name or even his face, but I remember jeans, a black cowboy shirt with white detailing, and a big black cowboy hat. We had no relationship whatsoever except that we would dance with him. He really only existed in that room and has become Charlie to me, the leading man in my song.

I wanted to tie the stories of Charlie Lake I had collected in my mind, the mystique, the history, into my experience, but mostly to pay tribute to the two major stories of spirits at the lake: the caves and the men who drowned while building the Alaska Highway. In my mind, the Northern Lights were the souls who were eternally connected there, attempting to jump from the sky and live again, through me, through my friends, through our whistles. In my mind, I connected the dancing lights to my love of two-step dancing in the area, the only dancing I've ever personally connected with and loved.

I wrote "Charlie Lake" over several days in September of 2011. The work I was doing at the time was very mathematical and tedious, and my creative mind would wander. At work, I would lock myself in the washroom with my phone to record voice memos of my ideas and then work the song out at night. I'm very attached to the song, story, and visuals. The melody reflects the whistles I heard that night, and to me it paints the colours, landscape, and presence of the area.

In 2014, I performed "Charlie Lake" at Summerfolk Music & Crafts Festival in Owen Sound. Fellow performer Leela Gilday told me that many First Nation traditions believe you should not whistle at the Northern Lights, that the spirits will come and take your soul amongst them if you do. For a while, this made me wonder if I was risking my life a little each time I sang the song. But when I close my eyes and remember that night, I felt connected to the spirits' life, as if they were saying hello.

I haven't done much research since I put my song together. I like to preserve my experience and thoughts on some level, and this chapter does reflect my thoughts and knowledge at the time of writing the song. But I also love that this is an ongoing story, history that grows with each one of us, each visitor and each display of Aurora Borealis.

Through writing this chapter, I've learned that the Charlie Lake Caves are now called Tse'KWa and are privately owned by Treaty 8. They were purchased just after I wrote my song, on May 29, 2012. This makes me so happy. There is contact information to view the caves online, and I hope you can do so if you're ever in the area.

TRUSCOTT

October 2011

If your father stayed a teacher
I would never need a preacher
To beg forgiveness for things I never did

If my bike had hit a rock
And never turned right down that block
Baby, there'd be other girls inside my head

No, not so much
It was only you
All the way through

I played a silent game with
Each and every single day
Thinking this might be the one where I forget

And everyday I wake
I hope that it's the one they make
The real arrest, but it hasn't happened yet

No, not so much
It's been only me
And no such luck

Most people let their memories go, from fourteen years old
Whatever were you doing alone, twelve years
And a lifetime ago

Money's never made a man
But I guarantee his story can
At the end of the day
It's a little bit of love that goes a long, long way

Never thought I'd find a mate
Or let alone even a date
Who'd see all of these things I am
And give me love

I tried to steer this future
Sew up all these wounds with sutures
But does anybody choose what they become?

No, not too much
I think we all adjust
In God we trust

Most people let their memories go, from fourteen years old
Whatever were you doing alone, twelve years
And a lifetime ago

Money's never made a man
But I guarantee his story can
At the end of the day
It's a little bit of love that goes a long, long way
A little bit of love goes a long, long way

☽○☾

TRUSCOTT

The idea for Trent Severn came my way just after I had written "Charlie Lake." I had played a show in Sarnia that year with area native Emm Gryner. She had an idea for an all-female Canadiana trio in the vein of Crosby, Stills, Nash, and Young meets Stompin' Tom Connors, and I was all in. Being a solo singer-songwriter is lonely at times, and I was ready for some coworkers and a new adventure.

As soon as we started talking about the Canadiana themes and ideas we would present with this project, I knew I wanted to contribute a song about the Steven Truscott story. "Truscott" would be the first song I penned for our debut album, the eponymous *Trent Severn*.

I first read the *The Steven Truscott Story* when I was thirteen. I know this because I remember I was exactly the age between Lynne Harper, twelve and Steven Truscott, fourteen. I just couldn't believe that someone one year younger than me lost her life, and that someone one year older than me was convicted of murder and sentenced to die, all less than an hour away from where I grew up.

I purchased the book again in 2011 and reread it in preparation for writing my song. I had closely followed Steven's story over the years, catching specials on television about the case and reading news articles, but I really wanted to write the song from what I imagined would be Steven's perspective. He coauthored *The Steven Truscott Story* with Bill Trent, and that would be the window through which I would try to fix my

point of view. It was also important to me to create a piece that reflected my emotions regarding the case. Steven was officially acquitted in 2007 and in 2008 was awarded $6.5 million in compensation.

For the song, I used details from his book to examine the emotions of an innocent young man. How many times would he have gone over that night in his head, regretting the timing of where he was that evening, examining how he could have changed each of his actions to alter the outcome? When would this turn into waking each day, wondering if the real suspect had been caught? And when do you give up on that idea? How many days, months, years does that take? I of course couldn't stop thinking about the life Lynne Harper would never lead and how much heartbreak her family had endured. How often did Steven think of her each day? I was also amazed that Steven was able to establish the life he has for himself, against all odds, a relatively quiet life with a family in Southern Ontario. This was something I still hadn't managed to do at thirty-three, despite there being no huge roadblocks in my life.

I performed the song for the first time in October of 2011 at the North Peace Cultural Centre in Fort St. John at a show of local songwriters, each sharing one song. I had also recently written "Charlie Lake," and it was reflective of the area, so I decided to perform that song. During the show we got word that our good friend and fellow songwriter Ryan Hennessey wasn't going to be able to play because his daughter had just fallen off a horse, and he rushed to the hospital to be by her side. She was okay, but I know we were all really concerned. The event organizers asked me to play another song, and I decided to try out "Truscott" for the first time.

Songs are never finished until you perform them in front of an audience. You can instantly feel what's not working in a composition when a crowd is closely listening. Performing the song is usually the last step of problem solving a song for me. I consider songwriting 25 percent good idea, 25 percent research, and 50 percent problem-solving over many days. The exception is the rare song that just seems to channel through you. Those are golden.

A fellow named Dave Constable approached me after the performance. I couldn't believe what he was telling me. Dave lived near Clinton, Ontario, and attended school with the Truscotts and the Harpers in 1959. He was seventeen years old then and was friends with Barry Harper, Lynne's older brother. Dave remembers being on the school bus on June 10, 1959, when Barry mentioned that Lynne "ran off" the night before. Dave also remembers playing volleyball in the front yard of his family home with Steven and others on the evening of June 10th or 11th, after Lynne disappeared and before Steven was taken into custody. When Steven was picked up by the RCMP on the 12th, Dave thought back to that evening, thinking he really had his doubts that Steven was guilty based on his demeanour. Steven was too carefree to have just been through such an ordeal and certainly didn't give signs that anything was wrong, in Dave's opinion.

Compelled by the song, Dave actually contacted Steven Truscott and told him about it. Through email, he said Steven had okayed sending me an email address to share the song, but the address was not included in the email, and I never replied and asked for it. I didn't pursue it for some reason. I was afraid to go there, to be honest. Sometimes I'm not certain where my boundaries are as a songwriter, and although I loved this song, I wasn't quite sure if I should or shouldn't have written it in that moment. I was certainly surprised by the excitement and support it received right away.

Meeting Dave that night was very special to me. I could hardly believe that the very first time I ever played "Truscott," in a remote community in Northern British Columbia, Steven himself was almost instantly aware of my efforts. I felt good about this. I really enjoyed meeting and conversing with Dave and have kept in contact since. He is a wise and compassionate man who has seen a lot in his days, and I've been glad to know Dave in the small way I have.

We recorded the first Trent Severn record over the next year, all working together to create the project any way we could, on a very small budget. We included "Truscott" on the album, which made its debut on November 6, 2012. I remember a lot of folks around me wondering how and when I had even worked on this project as I was working full-time in Fort St. John that year. I really did keep Trent Severn a secret until it actually was real. I never know if an artistic endeavour is going to work out, and it's for my own good not to get too excited until it actually exists.

To support the release, we booked a series of shows in Ontario that kicked off at the London Music Club. Owner and fellow musician Pete Denomme graciously let us make our first appearance at his place, and to our surprise it sold out! I guess everyone was curious about what Laura C. Bates, Emm Gryner, and I had been up to. We only had a dozen or so songs and performed all of them, padding the set with tunes from our respective solo careers.

A man in his forties approached me after the performance, quite upset about the song. He said his uncle was one of the alternative suspects in the murder of Lynne Harper and that it had caused his family a lot of turmoil over the years. I do think he mentioned something about the mysterious Chevrolet Steven Truscott reported seeing Lynne get into on Highway 8. I became very aware of the negative reactions this song could evoke after that show. I found it amazing that I received such opposing, immediate reactions to the song in its infancy. It affirmed how deeply the controversy of this story was woven into the fabric of our community.

The next adventure this song would go on was beyond my wildest imagination. My bandmate Emm Gryner is friends with beloved Canadian astronaut Colonel Chris Hadfield. They grew up in the same area, near Sarnia, Ontario. In 2003, Emm released a song about Hadfield, titled "Christopher," upon the suggestion of a fellow Sarnia resident. It's one of my favourites of Emm's songs, and she and Chris have become quite close since then.

Just before our album was released, Emm sent us all a note saying that Chris's NASA support folks in Houston were uploading our Trent Severn album for listening while Chris was aboard the International Space Station. He was about to join Expedition 34. I just couldn't believe something I helped create would soon be bobbing among the stars. In late December, Emm forwarded an email from Chris: *I listened to your whole TS album today. So exquisite, it stopped me from doing anything else. You three are magic. I'm a fan.*

He chose "Truscott" as a standout for him from the record. He mentioned the song a few times in the press and added it to some digital playlists he curated for CBC and Spotify. This meant so much to me.

Chris is a folk music fan and a fantastic musician himself, along with his brother, Dave Hadfield. I personally think Dave is a great folk writer, with clear standouts like his song "Caroline," which Chris would later record on his 2015 album, *Space Sessions*.

While Chris was in space, he had been posting breathtaking photos and videos of our planet, and most of us earthlings were hanging on his every tweet. In early March 2013, Chris asked if he could call in to one of our concerts from space. We were all thrilled. He was about to become the commander of ISS for Expedition 35, and Canada couldn't have been prouder. We had a few dates on the horizon and chose our concert for the next Friday at the East Street Station in Goderich, Ontario, as our target rendezvous. We planned to perform his choice cut, "Truscott," for him, since we felt the audience would feel geographically and emotionally close to the song. Goderich was less than twenty-five kilometres from the scene of Lynne Harper's death and blocks from where Steven was sentenced to death at the Goderich Supreme Court of Ontario.

Preparing for the concert was so nerve-wracking and fun. We allowed extra time at soundcheck to test phone calls from each other over the PA system. Our soundman Darryl even had a special direct box (or "DI" box — a tool for converting unbalanced or high-impedance instrument signals into a format suitable for a mixing console) labelled "International Space Station" connected to a headphone jack ready for the call. We would later playfully argue who would use that labelled DI box for our instruments at future shows.

After soundcheck, Laura, Emm, and I went out for dinner at West Street Willy's downtown. With the courthouse almost in view, we penned questions for Hadfield we thought the audience would enjoy. Both Emm and Laura wanted me to do the talking, and although hesitant, since I suffer from some social anxiety, I really wanted to do it. I'd never spoken to Hadfield in my life at that point, and don't think I've ever wanted to do a better job at something. We came up with a list of serious and not-so-serious questions, and I made a solid plan to go with the flow.

Emm provided both my phone number and Laura's to Hadfield. I can't remember why. Maybe her phone was acting funny or something. Anyhow,

as we played the show, Darryl's partner, Karen, was manning the cell phones. We pencilled in which song we thought Chris would call after based on time, and he actually called in right on schedule. He called my number first, I guess, and it went to voicemail. I still find it hilarious that I missed a call from space and have saved the voicemail he left to this day: *Hey, Dayna, it's Chris Hadfield on the space station. Trying to reach you guys while you're in concert, patched through, but so far no luck. We've had a very busy week up here and things are going great. But hopefully you're doing okay, and I will try the other number also. Take care and hi to the band.*

Karen flagged us between songs and passed Laura's phone up to the stage with Chris on the line. There was a bit of fumbling around getting the phone connected, but the thrill of hearing Chris's voice come through the speakers for the first time was incredible. The crowd erupted when they heard him, since they had only learned moments before that we were all receiving a call from the upper atmosphere. We didn't want to excite everyone too much beforehand in case something didn't work and the call ultimately didn't happen. There was a delay of a few seconds on the call, and it took a moment to get the pace of how the conversation would flow because of it.

I finally managed to ask our first question: "So, what time is it up there?" to which the audience erupted with laughter.

Chris told us that it was twenty minutes to two in the morning. They just had a spaceship undock two hours ago that was to land on Earth in about an hour. He said he had taken over as commander of the International Space Station two days ago, and that this was the very first concert he had ever called in to. All I could think was *wow*. I asked how life had changed up there since taking over as ISS commander, as opposed to being a crew member. He said it wasn't too different but that he was in charge of final decisions and making sure the lights were off and the garage door was closed at night. He was so funny! He mentioned that he had also spoken to the Canadian Prime Minister, Stephen Harper, for a half hour earlier that day, and that it was "interesting." I replied that I hoped there was more space exploration funding coming, which he thought was very funny.

We asked him about playing guitar in space, and he mentioned that he was working on a recording earlier that day but didn't want to say too

much to spoil the surprise. It turns out it was a space version of "Danny Boy" he released two days later, on St. Patrick's day. One of my favourite moments from the call was when Laura thanked her father, the endearing Dave Bates, who was with us in the audience, for helping with her cell phone bill. I mean, who knows how much it's going to cost to talk to outer space? So adorable. We serenaded Hadfield over the phone with "Truscott" as he began to watch one of sixteen daily sunsets, this one over the South Pacific. I don't remember much else from that night, but it was certainly a night no one in that room would ever forget.

Little did I know then where this exciting connection would lead next. The next month, April 2013, Trent Severn was asked to sing the national anthem in harmony for the raising of the flag on Parliament Hill on Canada Day, followed by a performance at Major's Hill Park. Man, was I excited. I don't think I'd ever been more excited! I worked really hard on a new vocal arrangement of the anthem, giving the chord structure a folky twist yet ensuring the lead melody was as written, note for note.

We found out later that Chris Hadfield was going to be there too. There was so much buzz about Chris and what he was doing at the time. He was the first astronaut to make extensive use of social media, showing us all what our hometowns and places we loved looked like from space. Most notably, with Emm's assistance, he recorded a version of David Bowie's 1969 hit "Space Oddity" in space, and the accompanying video, the first music video made in space, garnered millions of views from around the world.

Chris and the flight engineers from Expedition 35 returned to Earth on May 13th. We concocted a plan to do a bluegrass version of "Space Oddity" with Chris in Ottawa for Canada Day. Over the next few weeks, "Space Oddity in Space" producer Joe Corcoran arranged a fun new version for us to perform with our astronaut friend, featuring fiddle and banjo, and I worked really hard to nail that banjo part. It was so much fun to spend hours practicing, dreaming of what the experience would really be like. And let me tell you, this one exceeded all fantasy.

I arrived in Ottawa late on June 28th. Through all of this, I was still living and working in Fort St. John. All soundchecks and run-throughs were the day before the shows, on June 30th, and we needed some extra time

to practice together too. Joe Corcoran also flew in from LA to perform "Space Oddity" with Chris and us. It was monumental for Joe, really; he had done all this work on the "Space Oddity" track, which was a huge hit, but I don't think Joe and Chris had ever met until this event.

Joe, Laura, and Emm all arrived on July 29th. I remember the four of us cramming into the hotel room Laura and I had at the Quality Inn on Rideau Street, practicing. Joe would sing and play Chris's part. At one point we called him to say hello on speakerphone. The excitement built.

On June 30th, Joe, Laura, and I met Hadfield for the first time when we ran the tune onstage at Major's Hill Park. Security was tight, and I don't think we were even allowed to bring our families with us. He was striking, clean-cut and fit, and I remember his excitement, remarking, "The only band in the world covering 'Space Oddity' with a fiddle, a banjo, and an astronaut." He gave us Hadfield patches for our jackets and guitar picks with his logo on them. I may as well have been a ten-year-old superfan. Chris brought NASA astronaut Tom Marshburn with him, the first flight engineer from Expedition 35, and Tom was lovely also.

Trent Severn's schedule for Canada Day was as follows:

- 9:30 "O Canada" Flag-Raising Ceremony, Parliament Hill
- 3:30 "Space Oddity" with Chris Hadfield, Major's Hill Park
- 8:00 Full Trent Severn Set, Major's Hill Park

We rose early to get prepared for one of the most memorable days of our life. As we were getting ready, I remember Laura coming out of the bathroom saying we would never believe the email she just received. It was from Captain Steve MacDonald of the Canadian Forces Snowbird Demonstration Team. It said something to the effect of, *Hey, girls, we heard you wrote a song for us! We'd love to connect. We're in town also today, let's meet up to watch the fireworks on the Hill tonight*. A friend of Laura's who had participated in an airshow with the Snowbirds near London, Ontario in the days before had told Steve about us and passed on her email.

FREEDOM

December 2011

Baby, strong and free can leave you with doubt
When it's on the rocks you gotta get out
But when the night is long and the son's command low
You gotta close your eyes and get on the go

Freedom is a province of mind
You gotta have time
Freedom spread it out far and wide
You gotta be kind

Under, over, through gets you off your track
In a day or four you can always get back
And when they wanna know your home and native land
Just tell them all about, the cat will be out

Freedom is a province of mind
You gotta have time
Freedom spread it out far and wide
You gotta be kind

Wear your maple mind, your snowy soul, and your glowing heart wherever you go

Freedom is a province of mind
You gotta have time
Freedom spread it out far and wide
You gotta be kind

FREEDOM

The second song I wrote for the debut Trent Severn record was titled "Freedom." It was inspired while on a trip to Hawaii, where I kept running into other Canadians. I swear we would just would look at each other and know we were both Canadian, and I'm pretty sure this is a thing around the world. I had also decided on this trip that I wanted to reclaim the word "freedom," since in my opinion the U.S. has overmarketed that word for too many years, and frankly, I was feeling freer being Canadian there. On that trip I became totally obsessed with the local music and spent a lot of my time dissecting the intricate vocal harmonies wafting from the public radio station.

A few years earlier, when I was singing "O Canada" at the Fort St. John airshow, I met the Canadian Forces 431 Air Demonstration Squadron, because one of them, Lieutenant-Colonel Mike French, was actually a fan of mine from Winnipeg. He had even attended one of my shows there with his wife. Mike instantly recognized me and introduced himself. It was thrilling to be recognized by a Snowbird while hiding out on the Alaska Highway, since I pretty much enjoyed anonymity up there. Mike was kind enough to introduce me to the entire team and mentioned they fly to a lot of Canadian music. The Snowbirds line airfields with PA systems and perform their synchronized stunts to a predetermined playlist. He told me to keep the team in mind if I was ever writing something that could work for them to fly to. Well to me,

"Freedom" was the inspiration and song, so I simply dedicated it to them on our album sleeve and took no more action than that. When our album came out in November 2012, Lt.-Col. French was no longer on the team because members rotate out every few years. So you can imagine how thrilled I was that the dedication had made it to the Snowbirds simply by word of mouth in 2013. By the end of July that year, the story would return full circle when I watched the CF Snowbirds fly to my song in Fort St. John, just as I had dreamed of doing since Mike planted the seed years earlier.

Anyhow, back to July 1, 2013. It was going to be a long Canada Day. We calmed ourselves down after we read the email from Captain MacDonald and focused on the tasks at hand: sing the anthem perfectly on Parliament Hill on Canada Day. Play "Space Oddity on Earth" for the first time on Earth with an astronaut. All before dinner. No pressure.

The day was so memorable. I'll never forget how exciting it was to be waiting on stage, banjo in hand as Col. Chris Hadfield was announced, and the sound of the crowd cheering for him when he took the stage in his blue flight suit. Funny enough, the standout hour for me was dinner that night after the show with Chris, the moments when we could pause and reflect on what was happening around us. Both Laura and my family and friends all went to a little spot in ByWard Market and shared stories of the day over our meal. No one could believe what was happening and how exciting the whole experience was. To be honest, when we headed back to Major's Hill to perform our own set that evening, we were so exhausted that we certainly were not at our best. Too bad, but it was what it was. Our adrenaline had simply run out.

Along with my parents, I was especially happy to have one of my coworkers from FSJ there, Dirk Kuik. Dirk was from Holland and travelled back and forth to FSJ every two weeks for his two weeks on/two weeks off work schedule. On his weeks off, he would fly to various adventures around the world, and the company would pay his flight in and out. It was pretty much the same price to go anywhere in the world as it was from Amsterdam to Fort St. John. I remembered that he had once even gone to Easter Island for his break! On this "two-weeks off," he decided to

come to Ottawa and check out Canada Day in the capital. There certainly was a lot of buzz around the office that Trent Severn would be playing with Col. Chris Hadfield.

Dirk is a lanky giant who was always wearing the same thing: an absolutely huge smile! He has a lust for life like few I have encountered. After we were done playing our main set, Emm went back to the hotel. At the time her daughter wasn't even a year old, and she needed her mama. We took Emm's exclusive access pass — with her picture on it — and gave it to Dirk, which seemed to work for our purposes. I will absolutely never forget Laura, Dirk, and I wandering beyond the security lines up around the big circle drive of Parliament Hill, just the three of us in the dark. I think we had special passes for singing the anthem that allowed us to wander more freely than most. We sat right on the front steps of Parliament Hill and watched the massive crowd as they watched the band Metric perform with their backs to us. I remember glancing up and seeing men in black patrol suits hanging out on the roof of Parliament Hill, looking down at us. I think they were actual snipers!

When the concert concluded, we headed around the right side of Parliament Hill. There, we finally met Captain Steve MacDonald and the entire Snowbird team. Who could have ever imagined that the most exciting day of my life would end with watching the Canada Day fireworks over the Ottawa River, at the back of Parliament Hill with the Snowbirds demonstration team and two astronauts?

You'd think my crazy adventure of good luck and circumstance ended there, but it didn't. Trent Severn has had the honour of playing with Chris Hadfield several times since, and I've watched the Snowbirds fly to "Freedom" a few times now. Captain Steve MacDonald has even said hello from the skies a few times, buzzing down the Bow River when I lived in Calgary and running rings around my Stratford home as he arrived in town for the 2014 Stratford Air Show.

I must digress. We were invited to sit in on their team briefing and debriefing at that 2014 show. At the preshow briefing, the entire team sat around a large table in formation and ran a complete verbal mock of the show they were to perform that day. They reviewed area maps

and adjusted any flight plans as needed. They would then decide to run the high show or the low show based on weather conditions. Each pilot also reviewed three takeaways they noted from the previous show. It was a ritual reflective of the potential disasters they were not going to allow to happen.

At the debriefing, they watched a video of the show they just performed in its entirety and discussed it, noting three things they each could improve on, to be mentioned at the next show's briefing. It's truly unbelievable the insight we are granted as artists. This was certainly a situation I had never imagined being in.

Anyhow, I have to go back and tell you about the day after Canada Day, July 2, 2013.

I was exhausted from the most exciting day of my life, but Dirk begged me to stay in town an extra day to see the sights with him. I had a train ticket to Stratford for the morning of July 2nd, but out of character, I ditched it and bought another one for the following day. I hadn't wandered around Ottawa for a few years and was pretty excited to remain an extra day to absorb all that had just happened. We decided to make our first stop the National Gallery of Canada. We did no research; we were simply open to seeing the sights available.

So we walked in the front doors of the NGC, and to my surprise there was an absolutely huge poster of a piece of art that was essentially made in my garage when I lived with my partner Sean in Fort St. John. I truly was in shock. It was the featured work, promoting the gallery's Sakahan exhibition of International Indigenous art.

The piece in the photo was titled *Dragonfly*, by internationally acclaimed Fort St. John artist Brian Jungen, and it certainly wasn't my first encounter with it. The sculpture is a red five-gallon jerry can that has been drilled with thousands of tiny holes in intricate, interlocking dragonfly patterns. The care and detail with which the design was made resembled the traditional First Nations beading Brian watched his elders make. The holes represented the drilling for oil and gas that was going on in the area. When I first saw *Dragonfly* officially presented, I believe it had a light inside, which really accentuated the detailing.

In 2007, Sean and I moved into a farmhouse just outside Fort St. John that was owned by his relatives. There was a Quonset on the property, which is a large industrial garage where folks store farm equipment. We were not farming the land we were on; Sean's dad was with his own equipment nearby, so the building was close to empty and just sitting there.

That fall I received a phone call from Sue Popesku, the ferocious leader of the Fort St. John Arts Council. She wanted to know if the Quonset could be rented to a local artist for the winter. This artist was looking to pull his fifth wheel into a heated area and have a large space to work. I talked to Sean's family, and we agreed that the artist could rent it for $1,000 per month. That was as low as they could go, since it was huge and quite expensive to heat in the frigid northern winter. I was trying to get the artist the best price possible. I'm acutely aware of our struggles.

In moved Brian Jungen and his sweet dog Ed, the largest domestic animal I think I've seen. I seem to think he was part wolf. We would see them out walking in the field. Brian came up to the house once for dinner. He was so pleasant and kind, a truly beautiful soul. We all became circumstantial friends.

Brian has a unique story, which he shared with us. His roots are half Doig River First Nations and half European-Canadian. Due to a devastating fire in which he lost his parents when he was only seven years old, Brian was raised by his European-Canadian relatives but fully identifies as First Nations. At the time, I wasn't familiar with his work, but it became clear that his story and roots are embedded in the fabric of the way he sees the world.

One Saturday closer to the holidays, I ran into Brian at a local craft Christmas market held at the Royal Canadian Legion. He was holding some lovely hand-knitted mittens he had just purchased. I remember thinking that they were as sweet as he was. Brian asked me about an alarm system he had noticed at the Quonset, if I knew if it worked, and if so, the passcode. He mentioned that a mask he made a few years ago had just sold at auction for a lot more than he expected, and he thought

he should take security a bit more seriously because of this. I said I would look into it.

The next afternoon, Sean and I were working in the kitchen, where we often had CBC Radio One on. A report came over the airways about an artist from the area whose mask had sold at a Sotheby's auction for five times its presale estimate. Lo and behold, the artist was our humble Quonset tenant. I couldn't believe it.

The mask that sold was from a series called "Prototype for New Understanding," one of twenty-three masks made from disassembled Nike Air Jordans reassembled to look like Northwest coast Indigenous masks. I remember Brian mentioning that there were actually twenty-four masks out there, because he had to make an extra for Michael Jordan himself after his first exhibition.

I assisted Brian with the alarm and occasional supplies that winter. There were a bunch of tables and chairs stored in the Quonset that were usually spread out, almost as if someone was going to hold a community bingo game or something. Brian had moved a few to work on, and I remember the gas cans distinctly gathered around worklights. When standing in the lobby of the National Gallery, I remember thinking that people would never believe how unglamorous the place this was conceived in really was.

Brian invited Sean and I to go to New York in March 2008 to attend the opening of his new exhibition at the Casey Kaplan Gallery. We planned a vacation around this, and that's where I saw *Dragonfly* in all its glory for the first time. Pretty magical in comparison to the Quonset. After the opening, we shared a meal with Brian, the gallery owners, Brian's relatives Paulette Flamond and Gary Oker, and some local press. There we were sitting and conversing with the *New York Times* art reviewer, a situation I couldn't ever have imagined I would be in.

When we returned from that vacation and Brian had moved out, I distinctly remember sweeping up the little tiny pieces of red plastic gas can that were drilled out of *Dragonfly*, or at least its prototype or series mate. I was proud to be a tiny part of something so visionary and special in that moment, as I was again five years later, this time at the National Gallery of Canada.

Brian's work is remarkable in so many ways. It speaks to the assimilation of Indigenous art, the innocence of spirit, and on globalization and commercialism all at the same time. It is moving and important and worth spending some time seeking out and contemplating.

Yes, I know. If I hadn't lived this myself, I wouldn't believe it. But I certainly couldn't make it up.

FROM CANADA

Cowritten with William Lishman

December 2014

You followed me from Canada
And someday you will come home
I'm not trying to abandon ya
Just to show you what's inside of your soul
Oh your mama couldn't teach you ways you needed to know
And hell if I was gonna let you stay here and lay low
Oh you followed me from Canada
And someday you will come home

Sure as spring will come
And the waters rise
You're gonna feel a fever deep down inside
Follow your heart
And you won't get lost
You'll find me sitting on the porch facing south with my fingers crossed

I am always thrilled to take the air
To follow the whimsical lines
No video game can compare
No not even a carnival ride
And whether by coincidence or design
Birds have been here waiting since the dawn of mankind
Oh, to taunt us, make us envious
To cajole us up into the sky

As we fly wing to wing
I almost feel air like you
There are cosmic rhythms, our souls renewed
Follow your heart
You won't get lost
I am right here with you, by your wing, oh just look across

When I left you for Canada
I was missing a part of my soul
Never knew that a man could of
Been so kindred with some geese in a row
And that so many folks would hear our tale and reach out
It's been decades of connections through hearts with no doubt
Emotions stir so powerful,
They seed epiphanies and tears

And sure as spring will come
And the waters rise
You're gonna feel a fever deep down inside
Follow your heart
You won't get lost
You'll find me sitting on my porch facing south with my fingers crossed

You followed me from Canada
And someday you will come home.

☽ ○ ☾

FROM CANADA

In late November 2014, I attended the Canadian Folk Music Awards in Ottawa. The award show that year was particularly packed with performances by some of my favourite Canadian folk artists, including the Good Lovelies, Finest Kind, Lynn Miles, Lennie Gallant, and when Laura Smith sang accompanied by Paul Mills and Bill Garrett, who mic'd their Grit Laskin guitars with Shure 57 microphones, I wasn't sure if I had ever heard a live performance sound better.

Lennie Gallant played a song about Amelia Earhart titled "Amelia," with which I instantly fell in love. The music, particularly the acoustic guitar, felt like it took flight instantly as the song began. I remember thinking that I wanted to write a song like that. I later found out it was cowritten by another one of my favourite Canadian songwriters, Liam Titcomb, whom I befriended years before when he came to perform at Egan's that one winter when I was waitressing in Fort St. John.

I had a thing about flying. Due to a non-flight-related event that left me traumatized directly prior to a Toronto-Vancouver flight in 2007, I had experienced sudden flight anxiety out of nowhere that lasted years. It only started getting better in 2013 after I befriended some Snowbirds and an astronaut and was able to ask them every soaring question I could dream up. I have no trace of this anxiety as I write this, but for a while it was partial sleeping pills followed by frantic phone calls to friends and family from gate lounges to talk me aboard each plane. Because of that,

I became very interested in flight, since I had no control over my sudden anxiety, which honestly fascinated me even more. I know it was tied to that event and that it didn't exist prior to it, so it was PTSD of some sort. I also knew I had to overcome it. The song, "Amelia," seemed to soothe this part of my being and honestly launched what would be the final stages of my healing, writing the song "From Canada."

The morning after the awards show, I joined the continental breakfast in the hotel lobby, where I sat with fellow singer/songwriters Aengus Finnan, Shari Ulrich, and David Newland. David also worked as a guide for Adventure Canada. It somehow came up that the last time David visited Ottawa was to attend a Royal Canadian Geographical Society gala at the Air and Space Museum, where a fellow Adventure Canada guide named William (Bill) Lishman gave him an educational tour of the museum's aircraft. I didn't know who Bill Lishman was, so David explained. His nickname was "Father Goose."

Bill was famous for teaching flocks of birds to follow him into the sky by leading them in his ultralight aircraft. I had never heard a whisper about Bill prior to that moment but knew instantly that he would be the subject of my flying song. How completely fascinating and creative it was to fly with birds — and for his story to show up within twelve hours of my desire emerging to write a flying song. How perfect.

I immediately started researching Bill Lishman. Yes, he flew with the birds, but he was so much more. Bill was a sculptor, inventor, designer, engineer, adventurer, and boundary-pusher dedicated to the sixties mentality of finding one's own path. His career started as a metal sculptor in the 1960s and became wildly creative from there. In 1971, Bill created a full-size replica of the lunar landing module in his backyard. For Expo 86 he built "Transcending the Traffic," an eighty-six-foot-tall tower with eighty-six life-size sculpted metal figures spiralling around it, the centrepiece of the land transportation plaza. For a Chrysler automobile commercial, he built a full-scale replica of England's Stonehenge called "Autohenge" made entirely of crushed automobiles. He is the man behind the 40' steel iceberg at Ottawa's Canadian Museum of Nature, and he made the metal dragon and wild boar sculptures at Canada's Wonderland. And this list

doesn't even scratch the surface of his many creations. Bill and his family even lived in an underground dome-shaped house, which he designed and built himself in Purple Hill, Ontario, named after the viper's bugloss that bloomed in the area each summer.

Bill was also an ultralight aircraft pioneer, modifying and building many of his own aircraft. An early design was a modified biplane hang-glider equipped with tricycle landing gear called the "Easy Riser." One morning in the early eighties, he accidentally found himself flying with a flock of ducks. He described being so close, he could see the details of their muscles and feathers moving in the sky. It was a childhood dream of Bill's to fly with birds, and he was determined to recreate that experience.

Bill started researching imprinting on birds and tracked down celebrated wildlife and IMAX filmmaker William Carrick after seeing his Genie award-winning Imax film *Skyward*, which featured close-up footage of geese in flight, similar to what he had experienced with the ducks. With Carrick's assistance, Lishman successfully imprinted himself as Father Goose on a flock of geese in the spring of 1987 but had no luck coaxing the birds into the sky. It took three attempts over as many years to finally have a flock follow him airborne. The key to success was also imprinting the sound of his ultralight engine on the flock so the birds would not fear the machine when he led them into the sky. Bill finally achieved this by playing a tape recording of the ultralight engine as the third gaggle of goslings hatched. His dream of flying with the birds was again realized in 1989, but it would soon amount to so much more.

Migration for birds is not an instinct; it's a learned behaviour. If anything happens to migratory bird parents, their offspring will never learn to fly south, leaving flocks at risk of being wiped out by harsh Canadian winters. Bill wanted to know if he could teach the birds how to migrate.

Lishman teamed up with friend and fellow ultralight enthusiast Joe Duff and founded Operation Migration in 1994. Over many years, the organization established new migrating flocks of the extremely endangered whooping crane throughout the United States. The whooping crane is so endangered that in the 1940s their population numbered under twenty-five.

Upon the success of the migration flights, the American news show *20/20* featured Bill's story, and Hollywood was listening. The blockbuster 1996 film *Fly Away Home* starring Jeff Daniels and Anna Paquin was based on Bill's autobiography, *Father Goose*, although his family situation was drastically altered to accommodate the hired actors.

What really struck me about Bill's story was how this all must have felt. I mean, I did read somewhere that Bill would easily eat any trouble-making geese, but there had to be some deep attachments forming with the birds. I wanted to focus on the first time he flew a flock south to Virginia, and the obsession that must have persisted, wondering if they would ever return in the spring.

I was happy with my perspective for the song, but it quickly started to feel fraudulent and evident that I could only imagine what this was all like — which was certainly true. I wanted to relish the human-animal connection we all know well. I needed detail, and watching *Fly Away Home* didn't satisfy my thirst for this knowledge. With the first verse and chorus of my song written, I contacted David Newland and asked if he would connect Bill and I. On December 15, 2014, I called Bill at Purple Hill.

Despite my feeling like an unorganized kid interviewing Bill for a school paper, he shared some great stories with me. He said the birds came back on April 11th, around eleven in the morning, and that each year they returned on pretty much the same day and hour. He said the goose named Igor in Fly Away Home was named after a real bird he was fond of that didn't come home with the rest of the flock. However, Igor showed up a few days later with a couple of new lady geese he'd picked up near Niagara Falls. Our call sparked Bill to share a poem he wrote while flying with the birds, which he thought might be useful for the song. Just after we hung up, his poem, "True Freedom," arrived in my inbox. Three days later, I emailed the song back, which now combined what I had been working on and his poem. We tweaked the lyrics together and finalized "From Canada."

I'm a very visual songwriter, and in the first verse and chorus I see Bill speaking to the flock in his final moments surrounded by them after escorting them to Virginia for the first time. I kicked the song off with

the pep talk they may have needed to make it home and rounded out the chorus with Bill explaining the urge to return home they would feel so deeply in a few months' time. I tried to smother it all in the faith of a parent. The second verse is a collage of visuals from the air. I remember Bill saying on our call that he could feel every airy nuance the birds did while soaring with them in the sky. When I sing this verse, I am Bill in the ultralight, looking down at shorelines, feeling the wind, weather, and invisible speed bumps in tow with the flock. I imagine Bill gazing across the ultralight wing to see his loyal followers, taking in the view as his dreams came true. By the third verse, we feel Bill's gratitude for the experience and ache for the geese to return home. The final chorus and end tag redeems Bill's paternal faith once again.

We agreed that Trent Severn would come to Purple Hill the following Earth Day to debut the song at the official launch of Bill's new photographic coffee table book, *The Oak Ridges Moraine from Above*. We saved performing "From Canada" live until that day. It's very important to me that a song becomes part of the real life story of its creation adventure, if it has the opportunity.

The GPS wasn't accurate to Purple Hill on the back roads near Port Perry, Ontario, but we were told to look out for a metal sculpture of a camel that marked the driveway — of course! As we pulled in, we were greeted by many of Bill's metal sculptures, including "Transcending the Traffic" and other sculptures from Expo 86. Down the lane about fifty yards was the indication of a living space to the right and an interlocking brick patio that led to an entry hall on the face of a hill. It honestly looked like we had arrived at a hobbit's home from *Lord of the Rings*. How terribly exciting!

Folks greeted us in the entranceway, and it was clear this was a large gathering. First we were introduced to Bill's wife, Paula Lishman. Her blond bob and glasses framed her Scandinavian face. She had a long, small braid of hair twice as long as her bob that went down her back past her shoulders, and she was at least six feet tall. I noticed she was wearing a knit fur shawl, as were many other artistic women at the party. Some wore loose knit shawls in wild colours, and some wore luxurious, dense

pieces with whimsical details. I learned that these were all made by Paula and that she is a world-renowned fashion designer who pioneered Knit Fur, inspired by her upbringing in Goose Bay, Labrador.

We entered the house into the kitchen. We were in a dome-shaped room with white-plastered walls and wooden details. A round fridge hydraulically lifted from the island countertop with the touch of a button. It had a Californian feel, and I realized we were underground, inside the hill. There was a hall that connected us to the next room, a larger, round living room area with a skylight in the middle of the ceiling. There was a swing hanging from the skylight, and a million children were playing on it. There was a reporter from the *Toronto Star* there, some folks from Adventure Canada, and a whole bunch of family, friends, and neighbours. I finally met Bill, and we shared a nice hug and conversation. He was quite busy signing books in an office off the hall that connected the living room and kitchen. Bill was kind enough to gift me a signed copy of his book, which I have kept nearby on my shelf of cherished belongings ever since. I really was delighted by his large community of family and friends. Everyone was so comfortable together. No one in particular was playing host; everyone was just being themselves, managing themselves.

We explored the house a bit more. We saw the main bedroom because we stored our instruments in there. It too was a large white oval with Californian accents. It was apparent we were in a series of connected domes, maybe seven or eight of them in total. I think a lot of the furniture was handmade, and the oval wooden doors were accentuated with whimsical custom glass windows. On the other side of the living room, through an eccentric oversized door framed by wobbly square pieces of amber glass, was a half-dome family area with a fireplace and a breathtaking view over Lake Scugog. I talked to his son Aaron, who let me know that Bill was quite proud of our song, playing it in the car for anyone who would listen. That was such a wonderful feeling. Trent Severn played a short acoustic set in the living room toward the end of the gathering, and everyone seemed excited to hear "From Canada" for the first time.

It meant a tremendous amount to me to meet Bill in this way and to create something with him. I truly looked up to him as an artist who

pioneered his own life, and I was thrilled that I helped add the title of songwriter to his long list of occupations and achievements.

Bill and I kept in touch a bit after that, an email or a social media message here and there. I think it seemed like we were a lot closer than we were to me, because each time I perform "From Canada," I recount the story of Bill and his geese and in turn often think fondly of him. Audiences love the story, and I often hear more tales of Bill and how inspiring he was from show attendees in lobbies after performances.

In late 2017 I was crushed to hear of Bill's passing. He died on December 30th, surrounded by his loved ones at Purple Hill, just ten days after he was diagnosed with leukemia at the age of seventy-eight. The family brought a bed in for him and set it up in the far room overlooking the lake. Bill wanted to be at home but didn't want to pass in the bed he shared with Paula and leave her with that final memory.

I received an invite to his celebration of life in January and reached out to Aaron. I offered to perform our song at the celebration; I was hesitant, but I just really wanted to let him know that I would be there either way. He said he would love to have me play it, that many folks would be speaking and other musicians would play too.

When the day came, I headed to Oshawa from Stratford with close friends Cedric Smith and his daughter MadeNell McIntosh. Cedric was also once a guide for Adventure Canada with Bill and is a real-life folk hero just like Bill.

The celebration was held at the Robert McLaughlin Gallery. Many of Bill's sculptures, ideas, and memories were on display. The place was absolutely packed. Someone said they were expecting 250 people, and 800 came. So many wonderful and interesting people were there. I even met a family that was working on turning a rural church into a wizard castle, just to live in. I sure hope to make it there someday.

I was touched to hear Ian Tamblyn would also play a song. I think Ian is one of the best Canadian folk songwriters around, and I learned he also guided Adventure Canada tours like David, Cedric, and Bill.

My partner Keelan was living in England at the time and decided to join the live stream of the service. Keelan only knew what I told him

about Bill but ended up watching the entire three-hour service. The stories and memories shared were so compelling, one couldn't stop listening. There were really no better true stories to be told that I knew of. No one there wanted to leave. We all wanted to stay and hear more about Bill. I ended up singing "From Canada" at the very end. There wasn't really a PA, so I just played my guitar and sang through the speaker podium mic. It was incredibly hard to stay composed; even Aaron, who always seemed to keep it together, began to choke up. Many more people wanted to speak, but not everyone was able to. The celebration only ended because the rental on the hall was over. I will feel forever honoured that I was able to be there and perform our song that day. This meant more to me than any record sale or accolade I'll ever receive.

In true Lishman fashion, the family had brought an exaggerated life-size metal sculpture Bill had made of himself to the front stairs of the gallery. That way, Bill could greet and say farewell to each guest. Cedric, MadeNell, and I stopped to take our photo with "Bill" on our way out and said our final goodbyes.

Later that year, in the summertime, Aaron, Paula, and the whole Lishman family hosted a party at Purple Hill to celebrate Bill and spread his ashes. Keelan and I arrived late afternoon, just in time to join a crowd of a hundred or so standing on top of Purple Hill, watching an ultralight spread Bill's ashes all over the property. Everyone was smiling and crying a little, but the general feeling was joy. Bill's statue was placed near the entrance to the house, and I was able to say hello once again.

We set up our tent toward the back of the property and nestled into the various happenings. A little stage was set up to play, and Keelan and I performed a few songs together for the crowd, including "From Canada." A few folks spoke who didn't get a chance to at the celebration of life, and Aaron's band Boom Bust and Echo played us into the night. This band of friends was amazing. Everyone was up dancing and carrying on. I'll never forget the chorus to their song "Somebody Stop Me": "before I hurt myself, I'm not what you see, I don't even know myself!" At one point the whole crowd was dancing and chanting, "I don't even know myself," over

and over, and I loved it. I often listen to the CD they gave me that night and bask in the memories it evokes.

Keelan hadn't seen inside Purple Hill yet, so we decided to head in to see what was going on. It was pretty much a flashback to the day I met Bill, kids and people everywhere, but Bill wasn't there any more, which felt inherently sombre. The kids were all in the living room, playing on the swing.

That's when Aaron's daughter, Cadence, about twelve years old, spotted Keelan. Keelan's main instrument is the button accordion, and it was making waves through the crowd, since it's pretty rare in Ontario. Keelan is a great player who exudes joy. He made a lot of friends that day who were certainly interested in the instrument he was playing. Cadence approached Keelan because she also had a button accordion and was excited by the possibility that she might have found someone to teach her how to play it. Cadence would become Keelan's first student; they commenced online lessons that September. I know it brings Keelan great joy to teach Cadence, and she has already become an excellent player.

Last, we headed out to the campfire and passed guitars around until the wee hours of the night. There was still a crowd of about thirty people, some passing snacks, some playing the guitar, and everyone singing along.

Bill inspired everyone around him to dream and be themselves. He taught me a lot about how to welcome interested strangers into my life without judgement. He wasn't only interested in his own ideas; he encouraged and assisted others to realize theirs. I think I admired that about him most. The crowd that gathered to celebrate Bill was the evidence that ultimately, life is the true work of art, and Bill and Paula were masters.

☽ ○ ☾

I have another side story to include about this song.

Every new year, I select a few creative endeavours I would like to complete, and I pin them to my vision board. They can be big, small, huge, silly, or completely unattainable. Anything goes. In 2014 my list included "Photo shoot with Dave Brosha." Dave is a photographer from Yellowknife I had admired from afar for years. I would say his specialty

is photographing people in amazing landscape scenes. I cold-call messaged him that January to tell him how much I loved his work and about my desire to work with him. He wrote me back right away. He had seen me play at Lilith Fair in the nineties and was familiar with my music. Dave said he was hosting a photography workshop near me in the summer and proposed that if I would model for the workshop, he would shoot my photos for free. Done deal.

Dave and I became fast friends, working together on a few projects over the years. He provides photos for my projects, and I provide music for his. In 2017, Dave invited me to speak and perform at his yearly photography conference at his new home in P.E.I, where he relocated to in late 2014. The annual conference is called Land & See and sells out instantly each year. About fifty people attend a week-long conference packed with a dozen or so expert photographer mentors who each specialize in various aspects of the art.

When I arrived in P.E.I, Erin Brosha, Dave's wife, picked me up, and she suggested we hit a grocery store first so I could pick up a few snacks to have at the oceanside cottage I would share with mentor Renee Robyn. I distinctly remember a pickup truck full of potatoes pulling up to do a delivery as we exited the store. Yes, I was definitely in P.E.I.

I gave my talk on writing, production, and how to organize yourself as an artist in the afternoon then set up a small PA to do a solo performance that evening in Dave's rustic barn. It was a magical setting, and everyone cozied in for storytelling and song that evening. To my surprise, Dave had invited songwriter and P.E.I resident Lennie Gallant to attend, along with my folkie friends Suze Casey and Phil Hoffman from Calgary, who were visiting him. When introducing "From Canada," I shared that Lennie and his song "Amelia" were the inspiration that sparked its flame and went on to tell the story of Bill Lishman and writing the song with him. Well, guess who jumps up with his harmonica and takes the solo. Talk about full circle, once again.

☽ ○ ☾

Telling the story of Bill and his birds over the years has made me realize that just like the birds, we don't always have the instinct to go. But we all have one to come back.

Since writing "From Canada" with Bill, I managed to resettle in my hometown of Stratford, and I really do take a moment each day to close my eyes and send my gratitude out to the powers that helped me make it home. I no longer have a trace of anxiety boarding a plane and always make sure my return ticket is in hand.

Just this past holiday, Keelan and I hosted Aaron and Ivy Lishman, along with their kids Cadence and Deagan, for a visit here in Stratford. Cedric and MadeNell joined us, along with Keelan's family, and we all shared a beautiful afternoon of friendship, music, playtime, and food. I am very thankful to have connections with such inspiring people and am excited to watch Bill's grandchildren bloom into lovely adults.

Bill's Poem:
TRUE FREEDOM

I am always thrilled to take to the air
to follow a whimsical line
across the face of the earth
to carve wondrous curves
that skim rolling pastures
mimicking the forces
that formed a meandering valley.

It is bird freedom ever sought
since man could first imagine.
No computer game or carnie ride
can compare to the exhilaration
of gliding across misty hollows in the early dawn
or circumnavigating a woodlot
at treetop level
This is as close to bird flight
as mankind gets.

Whether by accident or design
birds have been here waiting
long before the dawn of man,
to taunt us, to make us envious,
to cajole us into the sky
to join them in their gravity-defying medium.

This is our instinct
this is the freedom
we have ever sought.
So engrained in the human psyche
that the image of humans flying
wing to wing with birds
gives pause to all but the most jaded.

The emotion is so powerful
many are brought to tears
once in that heightened state,
it is the time of epiphanies,
when cosmic truths flow
the soul is renewed.
This is our true value to mankind
those of us who fly with birds.

O SNOW

February 2015

O snow let it go, everybody knows
That it ain't good, to keep that all inside
Send it on down, blow it all round
Cover my porch and my car
I don't mind, no plans to get real far

How I love the thought of staying inside
Gettin' locked down with a glass of wine
Might be why I haven't moved yet
If I get real lucky my love will come by
We'll snuggle up and light this fire
And melt away

And you can do your thing
Without worrying
That you're gettin' in my way
Don't feel bad
Sometimes you make my day

O snow look at you glow
Sparkling under the light
Must be hard to be falling all the time
Everybody thinks you've been pushing us around
But I know we're bringing you down
The more I see of you, the more I know we've done you wrong

But I love the way you bury the past
Keep our eyes forward, slow down the fast; wherever we go
And you might sense a flake of resent
My back's been better and the shovel's all bent
And my fingers are cold

Still I try to understand
I know it's with forced hand
When you're gettin' in my way
Don't feel bad
Sometimes you make my day

You can do your thing
Without worrying
That you're getting in my way
Don't feel bad
Sometimes you make my day

O snow let it go, everybody knows
That it ain't good, to keep that all inside

O SNOW

I very thankfully made it permanently home from out west to Stratford in the fall of 2014. It wasn't exactly my plan, but in hindsight, I really do feel a divine circumstance of many stars aligning brought me back.

Trent Severn had just finished a fantastic summer of touring and appearing at several folk festivals in the Ontario area, including participating in the inaugural year of Kingsville Folk Festival, London's classic Home County, and the famous Summerfolk in Orillia.

That fall, I had dinner with a brilliant producer friend of mine from Stratford, Dave Kalmusky. He was on his way to work on a project at his Nashville studio, and his demo studio in town was going to sit empty for the winter. While I was figuring out where exactly I was going to settle, he suggested I move my recording gear into his place, combine it with his, and start to work casually on my next project.

I discussed the prospect with Laura and Emm. We hadn't put a record out since 2012, and we felt due. I would produce the record and engineer 90 percent of it over the winter at Dave's studio. We had absolutely no budget beyond what we earned ourselves, which was honestly only enough to cover the shows we were playing and to put a few hundred bucks in our pockets each month. I could do the project for next to nothing in this scenario. Our only costs would be some additional percussion, guest appearances, mixing, and mastering. I was working full-time remotely from home as a data analyzer, and this steady income allowed

me to volunteer my spare time to make this record. I was pretty lost as far as where I should be geographically at the time, and the focus of this project would be good for me.

Dave's studio is called the Blue Loft. It's in an attic in a residential house in downtown Stratford. The angled ceilings are painted dark navy, and Dave's careful lighting gives it a sanctuary vibe. I loved that none of my possessions were there to beckon my attention. My work computer was nowhere in sight. My dirty laundry was a few miles away. Music, and only music awaited every time I entered the space.

This was the first record I would produce on my own. I coproduced Trent Severn's debut and my last solo effort, *Folkyo*, and I felt very up to the task. I had to piece the record together. I only had two mics and two nice preamps at my disposal, so we weren't able to record all together. There is no isolation in the Blue Loft, so in almost every track you hear, I'm sitting beside the musician who is playing. Perhaps you can spot a mouse click or the sound of recess wafting over from the nearby elementary school.

I would start by tracking guitars. Sometimes I would start several times over to get the tempo and feel right. I find it very hard to record new songs that haven't been toured and played live. Tempos, natural musical pauses, and even keys must be guessed, and sometimes it takes a while to figure that out. And I swear that one can record the exact same song, in the exact same key and tempo, over and over again, and it's very different each time. When I've had the luxury of performing the song, I compile voice memo recordings of various performances. I analyze tempos and keys and build tempo maps for natural tempo ebbs and flows that support artistic decisions.

Producing for Trent Severn had a few upsides. One, the project had clear boundaries. Before we started the group, we came up with a manifesto, which would guide our creative decision-making. An important part of this was that we wanted to make records we could easily replicate live, which put boundaries on production. The tools we had were fiddle, bass, guitar, or banjo, three voices, and some percussion. Live, we were playing stomps and shakers with our feet.

Once the guitar takes were good, I would usually have Emm to the studio to play bass. She is an extremely skilled player and singer, and we could usually breeze through her parts in about an hour a song. Laura and I would spend a bit more time together working on the fiddle parts, but she had usually worked out her weaving bow lines ahead of time, and the recording was pretty easy.

Depending on who wrote the song, we would divvy up vocal parts. If the song didn't come in written with harmonies, I would often record and arrange all three vocal parts, and once we decided who would sing what, we would distribute them accordingly to be learned. We never sang our vocals at the same time; I just didn't have the capacity to do it, especially while engineering, but on some of the songs, like Emm's "Nil Visibility," we would double up the parts *à la* CSNY. I think that track had three of each of us singing our part to give it that unique chorused sound. I would say the heavy lifting on our recordings was always working out the harmonies and ensuring their perfection, which meant a lot of editing and post work too. I estimate I spent at least three hundred hours on that recording from November 2014 to March 2015, all while working full-time. It took a serious toll on my energy and stamina, as all records do. Shovelling the driveway became hard. Cooking for myself became hard. But this all comes with the territory of working full-time and trying to create something.

One of the first songs I wrote for what would become our sophomore record, *Trillium*, was an empathetic tribute to Stratford's celebrated musician Richard Manuel of The Revols, The Hawks, and eventually The Band. Richard was one of the most talented people to come out of Stratford but endured the demons that often come along with such a gift. In 1986, after a night performing in Miami with the re-formed Band, he took his own life. I read a lot about Richard, his upbringing, and the creative sacrifices he made. When I told Harry Findlay, the proprietor of the original Stratford sixties beatnik cafe, The Black Swan, about the song, he shared how Richard was amazing at sweeping up the place at the end of the night in its first year, when they were just kids. King of the background indeed.

When I recorded this song, I had an idea that I would like to invite David Woodhead to play bass on it because of his personal connection to Richard, The Black Swan Cafe, and the music coming from Stratford in the era that would birth such a local icon. Laura and Emm both loved the idea, and David took over the bass duties for the piece. I travelled with the tracks to David's place in Toronto, and we recorded the fretless bass he had built himself. David's sound, playing, and production ideas are one of a kind, and I was honoured to have him be a part of the project.

By early February 2015, the bones of our album were shaping up. I had a firm picture of how the album would flow, sonically and musically, but I felt that "King of the Background" stood out without another track sounding like it sonically. After sharing some tracks with Laura's dad, Trent Severn fan ground zero, Dave Bates, he shared with me that the album needed a song to balance the fretless bass and pace of "King of the Background." I completely agreed with him. Sometimes one song leads to another.

I headed to the studio that Friday night to see if I could get inspired. About an hour into my visit, I noticed that I could no longer see out of the studio skylight. Pitched in the front dormer window, guitar in hand, I started fingerpicking the rhythmic pace of the snow falling in front of me. It was so synchronized and perfect.

I was thrilled it was snowing. I wanted nothing more than to cancel a trip to Toronto I was supposed to take that weekend. It would build breathing room and relief in my schedule and allow me to get some rest I so desperately needed. I quickly recognized this familiar "snow-day feeling" and thought that maybe I wasn't the only one who wanted to celebrate this storm. Any good Canadian can find the selfish empathy for the snow day in their hearts. And so the song started.

The first verse and chorus came within minutes. The lyric, visuals, and melodies all matched, and the chorus captured the gratitude and sentiment I was feeling. I knew the snow didn't mean to thwart my plans, but man, was I thankful it did.

When I went to leave the studio, I couldn't even make it down the stairs and decided I would bunk there for the night. I loved how the traces of

my arriving footsteps and tire marks were completely gone. There really was no evidence of my arrival, and suddenly I had a gifted weekend of creativity on my plate. Settling into the studio futon, I imagined just how slow I would have to drive in the morning if I didn't cancel my trip, and how sore my shoulder was going to be when I had to shovel the massive driveway when I did decide to leave.

That morning, I wrote the second verse. I stayed at the studio again the next night and finished up the initial recording session. There it was. The missing song. Emm played a mean fretless bass on the track, Laura killed the violin takes, and there we had our sonic balance for the album. Deep down, I know that the Trent Severn records I produced and engineered were not the best they could be. I simply think they suffer sonically due to my lack of engineering chops, but sometimes done is better than perfect, and you have to use the tools available to get to the finish line.

Surprisingly enough, *Trillium* was the fastest CD to sell out at the merch table and made the 2016 Canadian Polaris Music Prize "Longer List." Hilarious. It was likely the most inexpensive record I'd ever been a part of, yet people seemed to enjoy it the most.

I've never written a song that connected me with more people than "O Snow." We all live in such a busy world. Not just adults, but kids too, and I truly think there is an underlying energy to most of my one-on-one encounters of a longing for space, relief, and rest. Sometimes the world is as relentless as a snowstorm, and you have to concede.

The winter of 2015 shaped my ongoing creation routine. Every other winter since, I have produced a record and enjoyed the fruits of my labours through shows and personal connections over the next two years. I'm so thankful for the sense of routine it has brought to my life. Winter is a wonderful time to hibernate indoors and work on recordings and art. I'm convinced it plays a huge role in the sheer volume of beautiful art and songwriting our country has produced. And oh, how I love performing "O Snow" in August. Somehow it works. It cools us off and centres our souls.

The *Trillium* album cover is a beautiful painting by renowned Stratford painter Shane Norrie. To say thank you for producing *Trillium*, Laura and

Emm surprised me with a similar gorgeous painting by Shane at our record release show. Shane agreed to commission it for them at cost, and it is absolutely my favourite thing hanging in my home. Thank you, my friends. Love is so much better than money.

NEWFOUNDMAN

October 2016

You're a cigarette, you're a wildcat
You're no regrets, you're never look back
You're a midnight, you're a wrong that feels just right

And I'm gonna miss you Newfoundman
When your heart returns to Newfoundland

You're a sneak peek, you're a reading week
You're a county fair, you're truth or dare
You're a skipping stone, you're a home away from home

And I'm gonna miss you Newfoundman
When your heart returns to Newfoundland

I know you're not mine, right place spare time
Never meant to be, but just what I need

You're morning hair, you're I don't care
You're apropos, you're my mother knows
You're play it again, oh you're all the king's men

And I'm gonna miss you Newfoundman
When your heart returns to Newfoundland
Oh, your heart belongs to Newfoundland

NEWFOUNDMAN

I remember the very first time I laid eyes on Newfoundman in the spring of 2016. He was entering the first dress rehearsal for my favourite musical of all time, *A Chorus Line*, at the Stratford Festival Theatre, for which I had secured two seats and attended with my father. We were sitting front and centre, midway up on the main floor, and Newfoundman entered across the theatre to our left with Stratford fiddler extraordinaire, and my good friend, Dan Stacey.

Newfoundman stood out. He looked old-fashioned. He had lovely curly, dark brown hair and a trimmed beard. He was dressed thrift hip in an oversized brown dress jacket, a nice Irish hat, and slung a canvas CBC bag over his shoulder. I figured he was another talented Stratford import for the season. Dan's band, Dan Stacey and the Black Swans, had been hired that year as onstage musicians for the production of Shakespeare's *As You Like It*, set in 1980s Newfoundland. I would later find out that Newfoundman had been invited by the play's musical director, Bob Hallett of Great Big Sea, to play button accordion with the group.

We are pretty spoiled by the talent that joins our community each year. With a population just over 30,000, Stratford is a relatively small rural Ontario farming city scattered with factories, yet it boasts an urban art scene that would rival anywhere on the planet. All thanks to the world-renowned Stratford Festival, which features four theatres within walking distance of downtown. Growing up here was endlessly inspiring, and I

know the direction of my life changed when I saw actress Lucy Peacock play Eliza Doolittle in *My Fair Lady* when I was ten years old.

I wouldn't officially meet Newfoundman until months later, in August of 2016. Dan Stacey and I had been working on a duo show, and our debut was scheduled for Friday, August 19. We played a mix of my songs, his original fiddle tunes, and choice covers to a packed house in downtown Stratford. It was a perfect summer night, and we were perched in the window facing the crowd inside. Newfoundman had snuck in the back door, and we met after the show. He was tall and handsome, with a dense beard at that point, and a freshly shaved head.

"Hi, I'm Dayna," I said.

"Pleased to meet you, I'm Keelan Purchase," he said.

"That's the best name I've ever heard," I said.

We exchanged pleasantries, and I proceeded to pack up my instruments.

Dan and I made loose plans to meet up the next day to watch the final Tragically Hip show. The Tragically Hip are Canada's most beloved alt rock darlings whose career peaked in the late nineties. Most Canadians born from 1960 on can sing along to at least a dozen of their songs, which grace Canadian rock radio across the country by the minute. Their lead singer, Gord Downie, who most consider two parts poet, one part musician, was diagnosed with a fatal brain tumour in the winter of 2016, and the band quickly planned a farewell tour, ending in their hometown of Kingston, Ontario. The show was to be aired on our national broadcaster, CBC. Dan and I planned to meet early for some food and get a good table at a new pub called The Hub in downtown Stratford, which was showing the concert on a large projection screen.

We met there late afternoon the next day. The pub quickly became full around us as Dan's friends Charlotte and Keelan arrived an hour or so later to join us.

Charlotte and Dan are vegans and don't drink alcohol, so it was French fries and sodas for them. Keelan and I indulged a bit, ordering burgers. I had a few glasses of wine, and he had some beers. He laughed as I kept running downstairs to adjust the sound to be perfect over the PA system, insisting to the owner that I knew what I was doing. As the night unfolded, we shared many laughs, songs, and dances with each other and The Hip, and by the night's end we had both significantly contributed to a sea of national tears as Canada mourned the end of an era of rock 'n roll anthems uniquely ours. It was an emotional roller coaster that we were quite happy to be on together, even though we were strangers.

I don't think either of us imagined how well we would get along. Dan certainly wasn't trying to set us up; he knew our age gap, of which we were wonderfully unaware of that evening. Well after midnight, Keelan and I left the pub and sat on the steps in front of City Hall, chatting and joking and taking in the perfect summer evening that I don't think either of us wanted to end. We started walking home, and when we crossed at the Ontario Street traffic lights, standing in front of Pazzo's restaurant, it became clear that he needed to turn left, and I needed to turn right. We had a moment, and before the moment became a memory, I asked, "How old are you?" I knew for sure I was older than him, but I had no idea by how much.

Keelan answered, "I'm younger than you think. How old are you?"

To which I answered, "I'm older than you think."

I had Keelan pegged for ten years older than he was, and he had me pegged at ten years younger. But I was in fact seventeen years older than Keelan. I adamantly insisted he head home immediately!

Over the next few weeks, I received an occasional message from Keelan online, to which I would reply kindly, but I was really blowing him off. We had so much in common, which made no sense to me, but I was unwilling to explore the feelings we shared on that night in August. I told my Trent Severn bandmates about Keelan, and of course Lindsay and Emm agreed that I should not see him again. Things like this just don't work out, especially since I was the atypical older woman, although my uncle was seventeen years older than my aunt.

On September 12th, Trent Severn had been invited by Lucy Peacock herself to join the Stratford Festival Company at their annual PAL fundraiser. You could imagine my excitement. I still idolize Lucy to this day. The theme for the show was the songs of The Beatles, and the sold-out show was at the Avon Theatre downtown. Afterward, some cast members decided to head a few doors down to Foster's Inn. Lindsay, her husband Ray, and I headed over too. We spent an hour or so on the patio with musicians and actors, and Keelan was as polite and charming as ever. Afterward, I told Lindsay that Keelan was the fella I had told her about. She was stunned. Keelan is 6'2" and looks like an Irish movie star. His knowledge of all things Canadiana/musical/folkie is unexpected, to say the least. Lindsay immediately suggested that I should maybe reconsider my position due to what a great match we were. He was not what she had expected at all.

That week, Keelan messaged me again, suggesting we have a Newfoundland jam while his great-aunt and uncle were visiting from the rock. He said his aunt was a painter and his uncle a musician. Well, meeting a family of artists from Newfoundland was something I could not resist, so we planned for them to come over late afternoon on Sunday, September 18th. I made a charcuterie platter, bought a big bottle of wine, and they showed up with a slew of instruments, including an orange Gretsch hollow-body guitar, a small amp, and Keelan's button accordions. I'd never really been around these types of accordions, although I remembered Bob Hallett playing one when I opened for Great Big Sea on tour in the late nineties. "Button," or "diatonic" accordions are a staple Newfoundland instrument.

We set up on the back patio and jammed for many hours. We shared stories and laughs, and Keelan even gave me my first button accordion lesson. What a challenging instrument, physically. My shoulder strength was not up to snuff to make it sing and made what he was playing even more impressive. He was a really good guitar player, too. I realized a few hours in that Ken and Trudy were not a couple, but brother and sister. It came out that Keelan's father — Ken and Trudy's nephew, Murray Purchase — was quite an accomplished guitar player too, and between casual lessons from Murray and Ken, Keelan had acquired those guitar chops. I just loved that he learned to play from his family.

As the hours rolled by, I guess it was apparent that Keelan and I had some chemistry, and Trudy and Ken made an early exit. I found out later they were well aware of Keelan's crush on me and seemed to fully support it, yet I was still not enthused. When Keelan left that night, we packed up the instruments but decided he would come back in the morning to get them. We had an awkward moment at the door, but Keelan went on his way as a gentleman. He told me later he headed downtown to drown his lovesick soul in a few more cups at Bentley's Bar with some friends.

The next afternoon, Keelan drove over and picked up his instruments. He very politely asked if he could kiss me when he left, and it broke my heart to decline.

"I'm not ready," I said. I really thought he was crazy for being so interested in me.

We did make plans to walk around the river later that week. As we circled the Avon, we talked about music, life, Stratford, Newfoundland, art, theatre. I really wasn't sure what I was doing, but I knew I needed at least to know him as a friend. It's rare that I meet someone who shares all of my interests and makes me laugh so hard.

Keelan only had two shows a week. I started calling him Mr. Spare Time. I had a bit of spare time too. I was in writing mode for Trent Severn's third album, *Portage*, which would be released on Canada's upcoming 150th birthday. Writing mode is when my schedule has a bit of breathing room to be creative.

We made a deal that we would hang out until he left Stratford for Newfoundland on October 31st. It was only a few weeks away, and what harm could come of two people who adored each other's company? Because of this expiry date, we were truly ourselves. We didn't tailor the dreams and desires we shared to fit a picture with each other in it. And I am convinced that was why our connection became very deep, very quickly. The truth and vulnerability were very present.

We made more walking plans. We went to live music shows. I'd offer to make a marinara sauce for dinner from my garden, and he would prepare the homemade meatballs. We would have impromptu jam sessions into the wee hours of the night. We were so comfortable with each other. I could even write with him there. I would go off on a tangent, and he would stop playing and let me work out my idea. I had never been able to do

this with others. He taught me how to accompany him on a few sets of Newfoundland accordion tunes, and I was overjoyed by this knowledge. He introduced me to bands I had somehow missed listening to: The Moody Blues, Emerson, Lake and Palmer, Al Stewart.

We went on a few trips to Toronto, one for Grit Laskin's Grand Complications book launch and one for Lori Cullen's *Sexsmith Swinghammer Songs* album release. He loved these trips as much as I did, and it was so cool to find someone so interested in the same artistic fare.

Every so often, I would see a glimpse of Keelan's age, but it was extremely rare. At dinner once before a Trent Severn show in London, Ontario, he accidentally quoted the chorus of the Barenaked Ladies song "Brian Wilson" as "Lying' in bed like Bryan Adams" — which we all howled at and became the inspiration for the lead track on *Portage*, "(Lying in Bed Like) Bryan Adams." A Moody Blues song he turned me on to titled "I'm Just a Singer (In a Rock 'n Roll Band)" became the musical inspiration for Trent Severn's song "No Anchor." He taught me to play a beautiful song full of Newfoundland imagery called "Have You Seen" by the celebrated island band Buddywasisname. I especially loved the opening chord. His influence was becoming quite deep.

With our departure looming, one afternoon while Keelan was performing a matinee of *As You Like It*, I wrote "Newfoundman." I had a lot of emotions going on that I needed to express. I was so thankful for the joy and companionship he had given me. I was extremely flattered to have a deep, thoughtful, talented young man adore me. And I knew that soon I was going to miss him like crazy.

The first verse of "Newfoundman" covers things that are enjoyable but maybe a bit dangerous. Things that are too carefree, possibly, and maybe not good for you. Like a cigarette — or perhaps the idea of a younger lover. The second verse lists things that spark a sense of basic joy and excitement, a week off from school, the perfect skipping stone. Keelan certainly sparked this excitement in me.

The bridge of the song acknowledged the independence, circumstance, and looming expiration of our relationship. The third verse embodies the softness and comfort I had found in him, and the chorus

recognizes that Newfoundland itself is always the other woman for us mainland companions. Of course, the title recognizes both Keelan's age and origin.

When looking back, the song "Newfoundman" all seems so planned, but it really did just come out. I didn't work too hard on it. It was simply true and sincere, and it was one of the songs that channelled through me. Once it came, I did the logical reorganization of the thoughts and intentions, and then it was pretty much done. The song starts on and features the beautiful chord that he taught me from the opening of "Have You Seen."

I played "Newfoundman" for Keelan the next day, and it sent him to tears. He loved it and was so proud. He recorded a voice memo of me playing it and shared it with his whole family, Ken, Trudy, Murray, his brother Quinn and mother, Maureen. It is a piece of art that embodied our adventures that fall and represents a very precious time to both of us.

One day in late October, I accidentally told Keelan I loved him as he was leaving my house. I certainly didn't mean to say it, but it just came out. It was the most honest first "I love you" I'd ever said. Of course, I was totally embarrassed, but the truth was that I did love him, and he told me right then and there that he loved me too. Shit, were we ever in trouble.

As his departure loomed, our hearts grew heavier. The day before Keelan left, we were driving home from an overnight trip to Toronto. We had left Keelan's car in Kitchener for a reason that I can't remember. We had CBC Radio 1 on, and the soothing voice of the late Stuart McLean was telling the Vinyl Cafe story, "Love Never Ends." That's the one about Art and Betty Gillespie who loved to share a Cadbury Fruit and Nut bar and two glasses of milk as a bedtime snack. In the story, Art tragically passes away from cancer, and three months later, Betty finds a Fruit and Nut bar tucked behind Art's side of the headboard. Keelan and I were so entranced by the story, with tears fuelled by our own impending goodbye, that we drove right past Kitchener and his car straight on to Stratford. We had to drive back to Kitchener after dinner to so he could pack his vehicle for Newfoundland.

I'll never forget my uncontrollable sobs on the front porch as he drove away in his burgundy Toyota Rav 4 on October 31st. I went into a deep

depression that week. I kept thinking, *wait a minute – I think that was my person*. But as sad as it all was, I knew for sure that I was doing the right thing, and that gave me strength. I only wanted the best for Keelan, and I thought that was likely not a relationship with me. We shared a few texts as he updated me on his travels, but we pretty much cut ties. I had sent him on his way with a care package of memorabilia and Stratford delicacies, and a Cadbury Fruit and Nut bar.

The very next week, Donald Trump was elected to be the 45th president of the United States. This was a great disappointment to me, since I couldn't imagine that making a positive difference in the world in any way. I'm about as far from a Trump supporter as they come, believing him to be motivated by selfishness and back-door politics, while fuelling his pseudo Good Samaritan plaintive proclamations with pop culture publicity tricks. Keelan and I had joked before he left Ontario that if Trump got elected, we would get back together, thinking that it was impossible. I really believe that the election outcome made both Keelan and I think hard about what was important in our lives.

In late November, I penned a song for *Portage* titled "The Jack Pine," in anticipation of July 8, 2017, the hundredth anniversary of acclaimed Canadian Painter Tom Thomson's mysterious drowning on Canoe Lake in Algonquin Park. I was pining for Keelan and channelled my feelings into pretending I was The Jack Pine standing in the wind, completely flattered that Tom Thomson had decided to paint me. I was equally as flattered to be loved by Keelan, and that perspective was working therapeutically for me. As I penned the chorus as The Jack Pine to Thomson, "I want you to be, the only one to capture me," I certainly had my recent love in mind.

By Christmas, we were both still afflicted, and in a risky decision, we made plans for Keelan to visit Stratford from Boxing Day to just after New Year's, when he would return to complete some casual courses toward his degree in theatre at Grenfell, the Corner Brook Campus of Memorial University, NFD. I think both of us were nervous about the decision, and there were certainly times I felt it was the wrong one before he arrived.

I picked him up at the airport in Toronto, and we instantly fell in step again. We played tons of music, and I decided he could meet my folks

on this trip. I didn't even really tell them about Keelan before we had dinner, followed by a game of Rummoli at my place. My mom enjoyed us together, and my dad was not immediately happy about our age gap, even though he liked Keelan very much and eventually came around. We hosted a New Year's Eve party with all of our mutual friends, and soon enough I drove Keelan back to the airport. Again, we didn't know where this was going but knew we needed each other's company.

Keelan returned to visit in February, funny enough on his reading week (see verse two of "Newfoundman"). At the time, I was producing and engineering *Portage* over at David Kalmusky's studio a few blocks from my house. I explained to Keelan that I was very busy, and he would have to bear with me as I worked. He had coursework to keep him busy, and we somehow managed to have just as much fun on this trip too. He would work at the back of the studio as I recorded bed tracks and mapped vocal harmonies.

In April, we decided it was time for me to come to visit him in Humber Village, Newfoundland, just outside the city of Corner Brook on the west coast of the island. I booked a short trip over Easter weekend. It was just Keelan and his brother Quinn at his family home, along with some university borders, because his parents had temporarily relocated to Doha, Qatar, for work reasons. A week before I was set to arrive, we learned that Keelan's father Murray would be returning home and would be there when I arrived. With our age gap in mind, I was pretty nervous about all this, even though there were certainly no secrets.

Keelan assured me all would be fine. We really hadn't had to worry about our age gap in a little while, but I guess I had to give his friends and family credit. Anyone who knows Keelan understands how unique he is, and they knew him best. Well, there were no problems. Instead of two peas in a pod, there were now three — Murray, Keelan, and myself, and it felt like a winter wonderland vacation. We made fires and food, told stories, and passed the guitars around for hours. Quinn and I even hit it off really well and have become good friends. We all went skiing at nearby Marble Mountain. Keelan took me to see the ocean and lie in the tuckamore at Bottle Cove. I thought Corner Brook looked like a

British Columbian Hollywood Hills surrounded by ocean and slathered in Newfoundland realness and charm. I absolutely loved it there, and his beautiful family home on the Humber River was a sanctuary.

Leaving Keelan that trip was especially hard. He had landed a summer job performing at Theatre Newfoundland in Cow Head, located in Gros Morne National Park. He would be there full-time from May to August and just wouldn't be able to come visit me any more. I certainly didn't want to trap him in a committed relationship when he had this exciting adventure and a final year of university ahead of him. I really thought that was probably the end of us. When I got back to Ontario, I was a little sadder. I remember mentioning to Keelan on the phone that I was unsure when I'd see him again, and always positive, he confidently assured me that he'd see me soon enough. I had expressed my sorrow to Lindsay and Emm a few times as we were rehearsing for some Trent Severn shows that spring.

The next week, just before my birthday, Emm texted that she wanted to stop by one morning and chat. I fixed her a coffee, and not too long after we sat down, there was a knock at my door. I could see through the glass window that there was a large box on my porch. It was for a washing machine, but no deliveryman was around. As I opened the door to inspect the package, the beautiful sound of button accordion began to drift from the huge package. I squealed as I folded one of the cardboard flaps back to see Keelan inside and squealed again as he popped out like a real life Jack-in-the-Box playing the accordion. I don't think I had ever been happier in my life. Emm's brother Frank and my childhood friend Heather Steinson came out from around the house. Man, they got me. What a thoughtful plan they had concocted. Lindsay, Emm, Frank, Heather, and a slew of my other friends had schemed together to buy a plane ticket for Keelan to be there for my birthday, and it was the best present I ever could have imagined. It was especially sweet because Trent Severn had a few shows that week, and Keelan would travel and play with us in Napanee and Newmarket. My bandmates loved his company almost as much as I did.

It wasn't until that trip, eight months after we met, that we finally had a chat about our relationship and what the future would look like. I sug-

gested that maybe we have an open relationship for the next year as he performed in Cow Head and finished school. I didn't want that but really didn't want him to feel pressured or constrained. He responded with an absolute no, that was not what he wanted, and he really thought that we could make it work, even though scheduling wouldn't allow him to visit me in Stratford again until Thanksgiving.

I managed to visit Keelan three times that summer. On the second trip, I was to meet Maureen Bradley, Keelan's mother, who kept her maiden name. She offered to pick me up at the Deer Lake airport and drive me to stay with Keelan up in Cow Head. I was most nervous for that introduction.

Originally from a family of nine children near Milton, Ontario, Maureen is a teacher and had spent recent years as a school counsellor at Grenfell and overseas. She is one of the great listeners, full of wisdom and intuition, and on that two-hour drive I somehow poured my heart out to her. I adored her instantly and knew right away that everything was going to be okay. She shared on that drive that she had thought Keelan had been an old man trapped in a younger body since he was five years old and that our relationship didn't really surprise her.

What kept happening to Keelan and I was that we would completely forget about our age gap, since acquaintances and strangers couldn't tell, and our friends and family were fully supportive. It was only when a new situation presented that we would become aware of being judged again. Of course, people have an image of what our age gap looks like in their head, and that image is hard to come to terms with, without the reality of the ease and connection that exists between us.

Over the years, that worry has passed entirely. I rarely think about it any more. Of course, it comes up when I think about starting a family, but that's about it. I know it's a bit late for me and a bit too early for him. But then I think when is anything perfect, and who knows if we will?

Honestly, there's so much more to our story that I'd love to share, but I have to end this chapter somewhere. Keelan moved in with me after he graduated university in 2018, where he was honoured with the Tommy Sexton (Codco) Triple Threat Award. I hadn't seen him act until that final year in university, and I have to say I was thrilled. He was brilliant, as I

knew he would be, and I certainly suspect the professors chose their fourth-year play, *Ring Round the Moon*, because they had Keelan to play lead roles as twin brothers who don't even change outfits.

We have so many great adventures behind us, and even more that currently await us, including a trip to Ireland this year with our friend Cedric Smith and his daughter MadeNell. There are many projects and exciting artistic endeavours for both of us on the horizon, and I love finally having an artistic accomplice to share this almighty life with as we support each other through the delicate privilege of being able to chase our artistic dreams.

Keelan Purchase is as lovely as his name. He is kind, talented, smart, wise, funny, and thoughtful, and I only want the best for him. I cherish each moment I share with my not so "Newfoundman" any more, and I don't care what anyone thinks.

I am so grateful for our love.

THE SAME WAY

July 2018

I wanna be wild and free
Change my tune with the clouds in the sky
I want to explore, isn't there always more,
To be seen to be had to be done

Oh, and everyone knows that you can't move on
Heading back the same way that you came
So I followed the tide, and the signs going by
And my heart never challenged the way

Until baby deep inside
There were needs I can't deny
So I turned this around, it was homeward bound
I headed back the same way that I came

Through stormy seas, windy rains, and steady breeze
Well, I knew my way back to these shores
Past younger days I headed opposite ways
Déjà vu, no, I've been here before

If you want to live on past the days you'll be gone
You've got to leave more behind then you take
And I could give up this fight, oh indulge in this life
But my heart knows it'd be a mistake

'Cause baby deep inside
There are needs I can't deny
So I turned this around, it was homeward bound
I headed back the same way that I came
And someday you'll go the very same way

THE SAME WAY

In May of 2018, I asked Dave Bidini, author and leader of the beloved Canadian band the Rheostatics, if he would write a short letter supporting my FACTOR grant application for my record, *Morning Light*. He said yes but that I would have to do something in return.

I had met Dave in the spring of 2016, when he invited Trent Severn to sing some backups for the Rheos at Massey Hall. Though we only joined the band for two songs, we sat on stage for that entire performance with a few of their other friends. The seven of us were strategically placed stage right as a human barricade so that the transcendently nervous and ethereally talented Martin Tielli wouldn't run off the stage. I was so transfixed by the artistic magic that poured out of Martin that evening that I didn't actually sleep that night at all. I think he left his own body during the show. I couldn't really believe what I had seen, and I can't compare it to anything for you. Let's just say that when I saw the most incredible Prince show at Massey Hall years earlier, I slept that night.

Later that year, Dave invited Trent Severn to perform at a literary event celebrating the release of acclaimed English author Ian McEwan's latest book, *Nutshell*. It's the story of an unborn baby narrating the overheard murder plot of his father from the womb. We were to present a piece of art inspired by the book. I really loved the book and took on the task on behalf of the band. I decided to adapt a song called "Save Me" I was working on for our third record, *Portage*, to suit the book and event. In

"Save Me" I was venting my environmental frustrations, penning the song as if Mother Earth was trying to coerce humanity to turn things around with an accepting, forgiving heart, but I was having trouble finishing the song. The perspective of Ian's innocent unborn protagonist was very inspiring and paralleled the absolute vulnerability of our planet in a singular, more focused way. This allowed me to narrow down my perspective, channel his, and ultimately finish the piece. The six-plus-minute folk anthem ends with an imagined category-three musical hurricane of destruction.

This latest Bidini-Manning favour exchange would entail writing another song, this time inspired by the Humber River in Southern Ontario. Dave's newest project, *The West End Phoenix*, is a local community newspaper celebrating Toronto's West End culture, launched in 2017. The June/July 2018 issue was themed around the Humber River, and I was to present my newly penned streamy song at the paper's anniversary celebration.

At first, I envisioned writing about native settlement of the area, destructive loggers, or a farming family. People, at least. I was looking for specific stories, and I was having a terribly hard time finding my way into anything specific enough to emotionally connect with. As I was doing research, a story about the repopulation of salmon in the river jumped out at me.

I learned that the Humber River was mainly populated by West Coast coho and Chinook salmon, which were successfully transplanted to the area in the 1960s. They were introduced when the river became overrun by a type of herring called alewife due to the decline of many types of predatory fish. The native Atlantic salmon was eradicated from the area even before the industrial age, in the late nineteenth century, due to overfishing and habitat loss. Despite efforts to repopulate them as early as 1866, attempts were almost entirely unsuccessful. Atlantic salmon can only be found in the river today because of a recent effort to restore their presence, but currently they are repopulated annually.

The salmon are born in the fresh Humber River, and they spend a minimum of six months in their natal stream before their body chemistry changes, allowing them to survive in salt water. Then they go with the flow, literally, out to sea, exploring the underwater world that awaits. But at some point in the next couple of years, an overwhelming instinct tells them to return to the stream where they were hatched to spawn. Folklore has it that the fish return to the exact spot where they hatched to procreate, and tracking studies have mostly shown this to be true. Through an incredible sense of olfactory memory, they fight their way upstream for miles, homing in on their nostalgic birthplace. The thought of the creatures finding their way through millions of gallons of moving, changing currents is hard to believe. The females lay their roe in deep-flowing river waters with optimal survival conditions, where the males fertilize them. The females sometimes manage to release thousands of eggs, covering up to thirty square feet. Then, due to the enormous release of corticosteroids needed to procreate in huge quantities, the bodies of the salmon start to deteriorate rapidly, and ultimately they give up their life within days so that the cycle of their species can continue.

I had a really great experience presenting the song. Although there were supposed to be three artists presenting original Humber River songs, it turned out I was the only one who had actually written one. And honestly, I barely made it. I had the verse of the song for weeks, but it just wasn't coming together. The concept wasn't working in the way I wanted it to reflect my own human story and how I related to their plight. On July 7, I had to be two hours away in Toronto for soundcheck at four thirty, and I was literally writing "The Same Way" until about 1:00 p.m. I'd never been in this situation before. Thankfully, the chorus came with huge relief, and the second verse decided to write itself.

I remember telling my Toronto friends who met me at the event that I was super unsure of the song because it was so fresh, and that I was considering playing "Charlie Lake" instead — at least a proven song about a body of water. They strongly encouraged me to go for it, and I'm so thankful they did. If I hadn't, I may have mistakenly scrapped the song completely.

After spending over an hour in this beautiful room teeming with some of Toronto's most brilliant minds, I was up. With my freshly scratched-up lyric sheets, I explained the perspective and gave it my best shot. It was the first time I'd even made it through the song front to back. I was welcomed back into the mingling crowed, but now people I didn't know wanted to say hello. And there it is again. The very best reason ever to play music: an instant connection with my fellow humans.

Oh, how I had felt the same salmon instincts flowing through my veins. I too felt like I couldn't get ahead without leaving my nest and exploring the world. When I found myself on my own in northern B.C. in 2009, many people expected me to return to Stratford immediately. The thought certainly crossed my mind, but somehow, I couldn't. I felt like the community around me was very supportive of my situation and that leaving wouldn't allow me to work through what I was going through with people who understood. That environment felt essential to my healing process. My personal battle to return home with a rich experience to share with my community and contemporaries couldn't be fuelled by retreat, and I had to make my way up my own metaphoric waterfalls I wasn't thrilled to encounter. I adapted my daily life, giving up a brand-new business I had started with long-term hopes of eventually going back to creating music full-time in mind. I immediately started working for a creative design firm full-time. I had to switch my focus simply to building a stable life for myself. Thankfully, there was no better place to get ahead at the time due to the booming new frontier-like exploration for natural gas in the area.

I worked very hard to purchase my tiny first house there. Eventually, I was offered a better job making schematics for natural gas engineers and a few years later a transfer to Calgary. I only saw that as one step closer to home. I sold my house privately by building a website for it and putting a for-sale sign on the lawn with the web address. I strategically purchased a condo in Calgary but ended up having the opportunity to return to Stratford within the year, while still working my job remotely. I eventually flipped that home privately from afar for a mortgage on a house in my hometown, on my favourite street. All while I continued writing songs, making music and albums, and touring. My ocean was full of opportunity, but the sense of relief I found in my birthplace was incredible.

I was finally able to slowly make the changes I so deeply desired in my life. I wanted to be in control of my time and energy. I wanted to have a guitar in my hands as much as possible, and I wanted my life to be more meaningful. I had Trent Severn and some savings to get me through planning what that would look like and decided do a 180 and start teaching music privately full-time in the fall of 2016.

As the lesson inquiries came in, I quickly noticed one thing: they were all girls. Girls who wanted to sing and play the guitar. Girls who came to my shows with their families. Girls who looked up to me. Their parents were people I went to high school with or had been at my last local show. I quickly realized that many of them were specifically interested in pursuing music because it was me teaching and within a week decided to focus and market my services to young women. Not only could I help them play guitar and perform, but I could help them navigate their feelings, their purpose, and express their perspective. I can feel the connections they're making and the confidence I'm nurturing every day.

After its inaugural year, I decided to call my business the Folk Army. I loved the contradictory title and started organizing Folk Army performances. The name allows the kids to feel part of a group and patrons to understand our mission and book us easily. I have expanded my classes to include beginner groups and songwriting master classes this year, so I can maximize time to reach even more students. I want to live on past the days I'll be gone, and I am determined to leave more behind than I take.

"The Same Way" is included on my chamber folk album, *Morning Light*. The album is sonically dedicated to my community of Stratford. The album title was birthed on my early morning walks around the Avon River that inspire my creativity daily. The sound is classical, theatrical, rural, pretty, and homey. It's truly an homage to the dichotomy of my city, featuring almost exclusively local musicians.

The idea was inspired in late 2017 when I was invited to perform with Stratford's INNERchamber Orchestra. The rotating ensemble is the brainchild of the brilliant Stratford-born, Australian-trained violinist Andrew Chung. As soon as we combined my folk stylings with their chamber beauty, I felt like I had found my home, coming from two classical musicians myself. My mom plays the clarinet and my dad the trumpet.

The combination of chamber music and traditional folk seemed like destiny to me. Chamber music has been described as "the music of friends" because of its intimate nature and was played primarily by amateur musicians in their homes for over a hundred years. Today, many musicians, amateur and professional, still play chamber music for their own pleasure.

The same can be said for traditional folk music. Created and performed by amateurs and passed on orally through friends, family, and coworkers, this music is still performed and passed on in homes across Canada today. It's the storytelling and refashioning of the music by the community that gives it its folk character.

Morning Light is entirely arranged by cellist Ben Bolt-Martin for violin, cello, French horn, and flute. Ben did his undergrad at Laurier University and attended grad school at the University of Western Ontario and the University of Wisconsin. He now teaches cello and chamber music at the University of Waterloo and has been a Stratford Festival orchestra member for almost twenty years. His creative genius has elevated and inspired my songwriting to new heights.

I produced the record again, but I made the sensible decision to hire New Hamburg-based, Juno Award-winning engineer John "Beetle" Bailey to engineer this one. I am a huge fan of his, and I just couldn't risk compromising the sound quality on this one without having a full set of tools myself. And the result is my favourite record to date.

It has taken me my whole life until this point to get on my feet, ready to be in a position to create with freedom, perspective, and stability, all while doing work I'm proud of and believe in.

There's no easy way to be a singer-songwriter. There are obstacles, roadblocks, and waterfalls to jump at every single turn. My next task is to incorporate the rights of the independent artist into my mission. As it stands, big data has infiltrated our industry and devalued our art. I feel extremely compelled to get involved in the future of our business to ensure the survival of my species. I made it home to spawn my own brand of creativity in my native territory, and I am determined to do everything I can to ensure it is not eradicated.

Funny. Here we are at the end of the book, and I feel like I'm just getting started.

ACKNOWLEDGEMENTS

I would like to express my sincerest gratitude to my publisher, Heidi Sander, who gave me the idea for and opportunity to write this memoir. Writing this book was an absolute joy and has enriched my life so very much. Thank you for inspiring me and so many members of our community. You are a spark.

Thank you to my editor, Allister Thompson, who is an incredible musician himself. What a joy it was to work with you on this book. Your insight, patience, and expertise are invaluable. Jamie Arts, thank you for making this book so beautiful. Thank you to Chris Hadfield for your ongoing support and for writing such a lovely foreword.

I have been very lucky to have many fans, listeners, and supporters who have stuck with me through the epic rollercoaster that is the music business and waited sometimes years and years for the next song. You know who you are and I do too. I love seeing your face in the crowd. My sincerest love and gratitude to you.

I am so thankful for the love and support of my family, David, Darlene, and Darren Manning. Mom and Dad, the sacrifices you have made are not lost on me and I know for certain have allowed me to follow my dreams of becoming an artist. Thank you for being so enthused to share this adventure with me. I thank my lucky stars every day that I am yours.

Sandy MacNevin has stuck by me through thick and thin for three decades and encouraged me to keep going at every turn. You are so special to me, and I am so lucky you came into my life when you did.

Many, many peers have afforded me so many opportunities to be creative. Thank you to each of them, of whom there are too many to list. But

I must especially thank all of my mates with whom I enjoyed many years of adventure and creativity with in our group, Trent Severn: Emm Gryner, Lindsay Schindler, and Laura C. Bates. I love our songs and memories and will cherish them always.

I must thank David Kalmusky, Michael McConville, Ray Coburn, Jim Scott, Deane Cameron, Brian Coulton, Dave Brosha, Terry McBride, Kevin Fox, Harold Hess, Sandra Kalmusky, Heather Steinson, Kid Carson, John and Heidi Bailey, Siegfried Meier, Sam Boyd, Burton Cummings, Brad Hernden, Frank Gryner, Mark Vogelsang, and Ben Bolt-Martin for so, so many things.

Thank you to my community of Stratford, Ontario. I feel loved each and every day here. It's incredible.

Finally, I want to thank my beautiful partner, Keelan Purchase, for your love, encouragement, and support. Your kind, playful soul is perfection.

ABOUT DAYNA MANNING

Juno-nominated singer and songwriter Dayna Manning exemplifies the very best that Canadian folk music can be. Her cool, clear voice, along with her insightful songs, represent a history of Canadian musical art that goes back to the early 60's and sounds equally vital today.

Manning's three-decade career has taken her from coast to coast in many forms, from major label recording artist to independent producer and engineer. As a modern renaissance artist, Dayna produced and engineered two records for her band Trent Severn, designed the Stratford Festival's bestselling 60th anniversary t-shirt, and produced the sweet sounds of chamber-folk on her 2019 album, *Morning Light*.

The memoir *Many Moons* is her debut work as an author, and she is already starting to work with several Canadian songwriters on her next book.

COMPLETED WORK BY DAYNA MANNING

ALBUMS BY DAYNA MANNING

Morning Light

Folkyo

Shades

Volume 1

ALBUMS BY TRENT SEVERN

Portage

Trillium

Trent Severn

BLUE MOON PUBLISHERS

Once in a blue moon, a story comes along that captures hearts and imaginations. We're a boutique Canadian publishing house that shines a light on diverse stories and new voices. We strive to have a meaningful impact on our readers through the books we print, and we are committed to publishing works that inspire, encourage, and motivate our readers to make the world a better place.

BlueMoon PUBLISHERS

WRITE FOR US

We love discovering new voices and welcome submissions. Please read our submission guidelines carefully before preparing your work for submission to us. Our publishing house does accept unsolicited manuscripts but we want to receive a proposal first and if interested we will solicit the manuscript.

We are looking for solid writing — present an idea with originality and we will be very interested in reading your work.

As you can appreciate, we give each proposal careful consideration so it can take a while for us to respond, depending on the amount of proposals we have received. If it takes longer to hear back, your proposal could still be under consideration and may simply have been given to a second editor for their opinion. We can't publish all books sent to us but each book is given consideration based on its individual merits along with a set of criteria we use when considering proposals for publication.